AF848118

Dispute Resolution Mechanism for the Belt and Road Initiative

Guiguo Wang · Yuk-Lun Lee · Mei-Fun Leung

Dispute Resolution Mechanism for the Belt and Road Initiative

ZHEJIANG UNIVERSITY PRESS
浙江大学出版社

Springer

Guiguo Wang
Zhejiang University
Zhejiang, China

Yuk-Lun Lee
International Academy of Belt and Road
Hong Kong, China

Mei-Fun Leung
City University of Hong Kong
Hong Kong, China

ISBN 978-981-15-1974-1   ISBN 978-981-15-1975-8 (eBook)
https://doi.org/10.1007/978-981-15-1975-8

Jointly published with Zhejiang University Press
The print edition is not for sale in Mainland of China. Customers from Mainland of China please order the print book from: Zhejiang University Press.

© Zhejiang University Press 2020
This work is subject to copyright. All rights are reserved by the Publishers, whether the whole or part of the material is concerned, specifically the rights of translation, reprinting, reuse of illustrations, recitation, broadcasting, reproduction on microfilms or in any other physical way, and transmission or information storage and retrieval, electronic adaptation, computer software, or by similar or dissimilar methodology now known or hereafter developed.
The use of general descriptive names, registered names, trademarks, service marks, etc. in this publication does not imply, even in the absence of a specific statement, that such names are exempt from the relevant protective laws and regulations and therefore free for general use.
The publishers, the authors, and the editors are safe to assume that the advice and information in this book are believed to be true and accurate at the date of publication. Neither the publishers nor the authors or the editors give a warranty, express or implied, with respect to the material contained herein or for any errors or omissions that may have been made. The publishers remain neutral with regard to jurisdictional claims in published maps and institutional affiliations.

This Springer imprint is published by the registered company Springer Nature Singapore Pte Ltd.
The registered company address is: 152 Beach Road, #21-01/04 Gateway East, Singapore 189721, Singapore

Preface

Dispute Resolution Mechanism for the Belt and Road Initiative is published! As organizers and editors of this Blue Book, we want to say a lot but don't know where to start.

The idea of formulating this Blue Book started in the fall of 2015 and then was proposed in the Second International Forum of International Academy of the Belt and Road, which firmly approved the proposal. Subsequently, a working group comprising experts from different countries was established. With arduous work of more than nine months and countless drafts, the working group produced the first draft of the Blue Book in August 2016, whereupon the Academy distributed it to the experts of the countries along the Belt and Road for comments and suggestions, and the Academy played an active administrative support role for the group. Although these experts are fellows and friends of the Academy, their active participation and tremendous support for the project were far beyond our expectations. They commented and proposed changes relating to the principles, framework, contents, words and even punctuation marks of the draft, which obviously demonstrates that the Belt and Road Initiative has won the recognition and support of these experts. We are very much moved by their dedication to and enthusiastic participation in the project.

Before the Blue Book is published, it has gone through more than a dozen drafts—revisions to comments and suggestions, and further revisions to further comments and suggestions, and so forth—based on the draft of the working group. Yet, there are still unavoidably imperfections or even mistakes in the Blue Book. It is our hope that it will inspire others to make further contributions. We are also longing to cooperate with those who are committed to this meaningful project.

The Blue Book is a collective creation reflecting the interfusion of the cultures, traditions, legal systems, legal values and legal thoughts of various countries along the Belt and Road. Without the slightest exaggeration, the process of making the Blue Book is a rare opportunity of education for us, through which thorough exchanges were conducted with the experts and we learned not only their professional knowledge but also their selfless dedication to profession and the principles of human behavior that they adhere to. We would like to sincerely thank the experts for participating in this project, in particular members of the working group. As a collective work, the Blue Book cannot incorporate all the views and suggestions of all the experts. We deeply apologize for this.

Throughout the process of formulating this Blue Book, our research assistants played an indispensable part. For instance, Dr. Haowen Wu often worked through nights in order to meet the deadline for publication. We express our deep gratitude to our young friends!

Last but not least, we firmly believe that so long as we are determined, persistent and united, the dispute resolution mechanism for the Belt and Road Initiative will be gradually perfected and implemented.

Zhejiang, China Guiguo Wang
Hong Kong, China Yuk-Lun Lee
Hong Kong, China Mei-Fun Leung
July 2017

Initiators of the Dispute Resolution Mechanism for the Belt and Road

Name	Photo	Gender	Nationality	Institution and Title/Position
WANG, Guiguo		Male	China	President, International Academy of the Belt and Road, China Eason Weinmann Chair of International and Comparative Law, Law School, Tulane University, The United States University Professor, Guanghua Law School, Zhejiang University, China President, Academy of International Strategy and Law, Zhejiang University, China Member of the "Recruitment Program of Global Experts", China
LEE, Yuk-Lun		Male	China	Justice of the Peace; Vice President, International Academy of the Belt and Road, China Honorary Permanent President of Hong Kong Commerce and Industry Associations, China

(continued)

Name	Photo	Gender	Nationality	Institution and Title/Position
LEUNG, Mei-Fun		Female	China	Vice President, International Academy of the Belt and Road, China Member, Hong Kong Legislative Council, China Chair, Hong Kong Basic Law Education Association, China
ADDIS, Adeno[1]		Male	The United States	W. R. Irby Chair and W. Ray Forrester Professor of Public and Constitutional Law, Law School, Tulane University, The United States
ADHIKARIS, Bipin		Male	Nepal	Dean, School of Law, Kathmandu University, Nepal
ALBERT, Daniel		Male	Spain	Professor, School of Law, University of Barcelona, Spain
BAIDELDINOV, Daulet		Male	Kazakhstan	Dean, Faculty of Law, Al-Farabi Kazakh National University, Kazakhstan
BALASHENKO, Sergey		Male	Belarus	Dean, Professor, Faculty of Law, Belarusian State University, Belarus

(continued)

[1]Names of the initiators below are listed in alphabetical order.

Name	Photo	Gender	Nationality	Institution and Title/Position
BITAS, Basil		Male	Switzerland	Attorney-at-Law, Member of the Bars of New York State and Washington D.C., The United States
BOLAYIR, Nur		Female	Turkey	Assistant Professor, Faculty of Law, Galatasaray University, Turkey
CALZOLAIO, Ermanno		Male	Italy	Dean, Professor of Private Comparative Law, Department of Law, University of Macerata, Italy
CHANCHANANON, Kasinnat		Female	Thailand	Investment Advisor, United Overseas Bank PCL, Thailand
COORAY, Anton		Male	Sri Lanka	Professor, City University of London, UK Co-Editor, *Journal of International and Comparative Law*, The United States
DONG, Xuebing		Male	China	Professor of Economics and Vice Dean, China Academy of West Region Development, Zhejiang University, China
FEDTKE, Jörg		Male	Germany	Chair of Common Law, Faculty of Law, University of Passau, Germany A.N. Yiannopoulos Professor in Comparative Law, Law School, Tulane University, The United States

(continued)

Name	Photo	Gender	Nationality	Institution and Title/Position
FUNG, Daniel		Male	China	Senior Counsel President, Des Voeux Chambers, China Former Solicitor-General of Hong Kong, China Member of the National Committee of the CPPCC, China
GIBSON, Brian		Male	The United States	Ph.D. in Law and Director of the Global Learning, George Mason University, The United States
GU, Minkang		Male	China	Professor, School of Law, City University of Hong Kong, China Vice President, Supervisory Board, Shanghai-Hong Kong Alumni Associations, China
HAHN, Michael		Male	Germany	Professor of Law, Director of the Institute for European and International Economic Law, Faculty of Law, University of Bern, Switzerland Director, World Trade Institute, University of Bern, Switzerland
HSU, Locknie		Female	Singapore	Professor of Law, Singapore Management University, Singapore
JBEILY, Halim		Male	Iraq	Managing Partner, Newton & Partners LLC, Iraq
JILLANI, Saqib		Male	Pakistan	Managing Partner, Jillani & Co, Pakistan

(continued)

Name	Photo	Gender	Nationality	Institution and Title/Position
KONOW, Berte-Elen		Female	Norway	Vice Dean for Research, Professor, Faculty of Law, University of Bergen, Norway
KURILOV, Vladimir		Male	Russia	Vice President for International Relations, Director, School of Law, Far Eastern Federal University, Russia
LAPUTKO, Kseniya		Female	Belarus	Lecturer, Department of Public Administration, Faculty of Law, Belarusian State University, Belarus
LIAO, Cheungsing		Male	China	Justice of the Peace Vice Chairperson of the Social and Legal Affairs Committee of the National Committee of the CPPCC, China Senior Counsel, Gold Bauhinia Star (having been awarded) Chairman of the Council of the Hong Kong University of Science and Technology, China
LIU, Chao		Male	China	Deputy Director, Legal Affairs Department, China Council for the Promotion of International Trade, China
LIU, Hao		Male	China	Vice Chair of the Joint Authorities for Rulemaking on Unmanned Systems Director of Aviation Law and Standard, Beihang University, China Deputy Director of National Research Center of ATM Law and Standard of China, China Hong Kong Scholar of the City University of Hong Kong, China

(continued)

Name	Photo	Gender	Nationality	Institution and Title/Position
MANICKHAM, Supperamanian		Male	Malaysia	Former Ambassador and Permanent Representative of Malaysia to the WTO, Malaysia
MATSUSHIT, Mitsuo		Male	Japan	Former Member of the WTO Dispute Settlement Appellate Body Professor Emeritus, Tokyo University, Japan Lawyer, Nagashima, Ohno & Tsunematsu Law Firm, Japan
MEHTAB, Farhana		Female	Bangladesh	Associate Professor, Head of the Department of Law, Daffodil International University, Bangladesh
MOENS, Gabriel		Male	Austrlia	Professor of Law, Curtin Business School (CBS), Curtin Law School, Bentley Campus, Australia
NEDUMPARA, James		Male	India	Associate Professor, Executive Director, Center for International Trade and Economic Law, Jindal Global Law School, O.P.Jindal Global University, India
PARK, Nohyoung		Male	R. O. Korea	Former Vice President and Former Dean, Professor of Law, Director of the Cyber Law Center, School of Law, Korea University, R. O. Korea Member of the Research Committee on FTAs of R. O. Korea, R. O. Korea

(continued)

Name	Photo	Gender	Nationality	Institution and Title/Position
PULLE, Austin		Male	Sri Lanka	Practice Associate Professor of Law, Singapore Management University, Singapore
SHARMA, Rajesh		Male	Australia	Senior Lecturer, Justice and Legal Studies, RMIT University, Australia Member of Global Research Center
SHETREET, Shimon		Male	Israel	Retired Professor of Law, Hebrew University of Jerusalem, Israel Served as Ministers in several ministries, Israel
SIPHANA, Sok		Male	Cambodia	Government Advisor, Cambodia Chairman of the Board, Cambodia Development Resource Institute (CDRI), Cambodia
SUN, Jungong		Male	China	Vice President, Alibaba Group, China
THEODORAKIS, Nikolaos		Male	Greece	Lecturer and Fellow, University of Oxford, UK Fellow, Harvard University, The United States
VERSCHRAEGEN, Bea		Female	Austria	Head of the Department of Comparative Law, Uniform Law and Private International Law, University of Vienna, Austria

(continued)

Name	Photo	Gender	Nationality	Institution and Title/Position
WANG, Chao		Male	China	Associate Professor, Guanghua Law School, Vice President of Academy of International Strategy and Law, Zhejiang University, China
WANG, Yimin		Male	The United States	General Counsel, Norman Window Fashions Co., The United States Attorney at Law, New York and California Bar, The United States
WEI, Qing		Female	China	Deputy Division Chief, Legal Cooperation Division, Legal Affairs Department, China Council for the Promotion of International Trade, China
WONG, Tim		Male	China	Barrister, Arbitrator
YAN, Houmin		Male	China	Dean and Chair Professor of Management Sciences, College of Business, City University of Hong Kong, China
YANG, Fan		Female	China	Assistant Professor, City University of Hong Kong, China Vice Chairman of China Affairs Committee, East Asia Branch, Chartered Institute of Arbitrators
YI, Lori		Female	R. O. Korea	Professor, Department of Law, Keimyung University, R. O. Korea

(continued)

Name	Photo	Gender	Nationality	Institution and Title/Position
ZHAO, Jun		Male	China	Professor, Supervisor of Ph.D. candidates, Head of Research Institute of International Law, Guanghua Law School, Zhejiang University, China
ZHENG, Wei		Male	China	Division Chief, Fair Trade Division, Legal Affairs Department, China Council for the Promotion of International Trade, China
ZHOU, Guping		Female	China	Vice Secretary of CPC Committee, Professor, Supervisor of Ph.D. candidates, Dean of China Academy of West Region Development, Zhejiang University, China
ZHU, Xinli		Male	China	Dean and Professor of Law, Supervisor of Ph.D. candidates, Guanghua Law School, Zhejiang University, China
ZUCKERMAN, Adrian		Male	UK	Professor of Civil Procedure, University of Oxford, UK Editor of the Civil Justice Quarterly, UK

Working Group

Chair

Name	Gender	Nationality	Institution and Title/Position
WANG, Guiguo	Male	China	President, International Academy of the Belt and Road, China Eason Weinmann Chair of International and Comparative Law, Law School, Tulane University, The United States University Professor, Guanghua Law School, Zhejiang University, China President, Academy of International Strategy and Law, Zhejiang University, China Member of the "Recruitment Program of Global Experts", China

Members[2]

Name	Gender	Nationality	Institution and Title/Position
DITAS, Basil	Male	Switzerland	Attorney at Law, Member of the Bars of New York State and Washington D.C., The United States
FUNG, Daniel	Male	China	Senior Counsel President, Des Voeux Chambers, China Former Solicitor General of Hong Kong, China Member of the National Committee of the CPPCC, China

(continued)

[2]Names of the members are listed in alphabetical order.

Name	Gender	Nationality	Institution and Title/Position
GU, Minkang	Male	China	Professor, School of Law, City University of Hong Kong, China Vice President, Supervisory Board, Shanghai-Hong Kong Alumni Associations, China
HSU, Locknie	Female	Singapore	Professor of Law, Singapore Management University, Singapore
MANICKHAM, Supperamanian	Male	Malaysia	Former Ambassador and Permanent Representative of Malaysia to the WTO, Malaysia
PARK, Nohyoung	Male	R. O. Korea	Former Vice President and Former Dean, Professor of Law, Director of the Cyber Law Center, School of Law, Korea University, R. O. Korea Member of the Research Committee on FTAs of R. O. Korea, R. O. Korea
SHARMA, Rajesh	Male	Australia	Senior Lecturer, Justice and Legal Studies, RMIT University, Australia Member of Global Research Center
WANG, Chao	Male	China	Associate Professor, Guanghua Law School, Vice President of Academy of International Strategy and Law, Zhejiang University, China
WONG, Tim	Male	China	Barrister, Arbitrator
YANG, Fan	Female	China	Assistant Professor, City University of Hong Kong, China Vice Chairman of China Affairs Committee, East Asia Branch, Chartered Institute of Arbitrators
YI, Lori	Female	R. O. Korea	Professor, Department of Law, Keimyung University, R. O. Korea
ZHAO, Jun	Male	China	Professor, Supervisor of Ph.D. candidates, Head of Research Institute of International Law, Guanghua Law School, Zhejiang University, China
ZHU, Xinli	Male	China	Dean and Professor of Law, Supervisor of Ph.D. candidates, Guanghua Law School, Zhejiang University, China

Research Assistants[3]

Name	Gender	Nationality	Institution
GU, Xianyang	Male	China	Ph.D. candidate, Guanghua Law School, Zhejiang University, China
HE, Xiaoli	Female	China	Ph.D. candidate, School of Law, City University of Hong Kong, China
WU, Haowen	Male	China	Postdoctoral fellow, Guanghua Law School, Zhejiang University, China
ZHANG, Wei	Female	China	Ph.D. candidate, Guanghua Law School, Zhejiang University, China
ZHANG, Xiaohan	Female	China	Ph.D. candidate, Faculty of Law, Hong Kong University, China Fulbright visiting scholar, Harvard Law School, The United States

[3]Names of the research assistants are listed in alphabetical order.

Introduction to International Academy of the Belt and Road

Founded in January 2016, International Academy of the Belt and Road (IABR) is the first research institution concerning the Belt and Road Initiative in Hong Kong, and is committed to setting up an international platform for academic and professional communication. Experts of countries along the Belt and Road from various areas, such as law, economics, finance, investment, politics and international relations, are invited to share their views and conduct research on relevant issues in the implementation of the Belt and Road Initiative. The IABR has held several international forums on the Belt and Road, and compiled *Essentials of the Laws of the Belt and Road Countries* Series and *Dispute Resolution Mechanism for the Belt and Road Initiative*. The IABR aims at providing expert services to corporations and institutions involved in the Belt and Road Initiative.

Professor Guiguo Wang serves as the President of the IABR, while Dr. Yuk-Lun Lee and Dr. Mei-Fun Leung serve as Vice Presidents. The IABR has an International Advisory Board with 26 experts and scholars, 42 fellows and 7 associate fellows from all over the world. The IABR endeavors to contribute to education and training of specialists so that Hong Kong could take full advantage of its unique position to develop international economy and keep world peace.

Contents

Chapter 1
The Process

International Academy of the Belt and Road deliberated issues relating to the implementation of the Belt and Road Initiative at its Second International Forum held in late January 2016. All participants considered a sound dispute resolution mechanism which will be the key to ensuring efficient cooperation among countries, their private enterprises and individuals along the Belt and Road. It was decided that a working group (WG) should be set up to formulate a proposal for consideration and adoption by members (fellows and associate fellows) of the Academy. Professor Guiguo Wang was asked to chair the WG and to invite experts from nearby jurisdictions to serve as members.

The WG was established with former Ambassador of Malaysia to the WTO Supperamanian Manickham, Professor Nohyoung Park from R.O. Korea, Professor Locknie Hsu from Singapore and Professor Rajesh Sharma from Australia as members in late March 2016.

The first WG meeting was held in late April 2016. In addition to the members mentioned in the previous paragraph, Professor and Dean Xinli Zhu of Guanghua Law School, Zhejiang University, Mr. Daniel Fung, Senior Counsel, Queen's Counsel and former Solicitor General of Hong Kong and Professor Minkang Gu of School of Law, City University of Hong Kong were invited to participate in the meeting and subsequently to join the WG. The meeting lasted for a day and a half.

At its first meeting, the WG deliberated the various issues of the existing dispute resolution systems relating to trade, investment, intellectual property and contractual differences among merchants. Professor Guiguo Wang introduced a paper on the existing system in connection with the WTO, investment disputes (investor-state) and commercial disputes (private party–private party), which also contains a general discussion of the merits and shortcomings of the existing system and a general proposal for creating a new mechanism. The WG then decided that for the implementation of the Belt and Road Initiative, cultural background, tradition, characteristics of the legal system and legal environment of the jurisdictions along the Belt and Road should be taken into account for formulating a new mechanism, which should comprise: (1) mechanism for resolving disputes within

© Zhejiang University Press 2020

G. Wang et al., *Dispute Resolution Mechanism for the Belt and Road Initiative*,
https://doi.org/10.1007/978-981-15-1975-8_1

each jurisdiction; (2) compulsory mediation; (3) arbitration; and (4) appellate system. Another feature of the new system is that it should be able to handle all disputes ("one-stop service" model) regardless of the nature of the disputes and the parties involved.

It was also decided that work should be divided among members to prepare a policy paper each for discussion at the second meeting of the WG in May 2016. Specifically, Professor Hsu would prepare a paper on resolving disputes within each jurisdiction such as national grievances mechanism, Professor Park would work on a paper relating to the policies of mediation and mediation rules, Professor Sharma would prepare a paper on arbitration and arbitration rules, Ambassador Manickham would prepare a paper on the appeal system with applicable rules and Mr. Fung would prepare a paper with regard to procedural issues in dispute resolution.

The second meeting of the WG was held in late May 2016 in the city of Hangzhou, Zhejiang Province of China. Professor Park informed the WG at its first meeting that due to other commitments, he could not attend the second WG meeting in person but he would prepare the paper together with Professor Lori Yi of Keimyung University, R.O. Korea, who was invited to join the WG at its second meeting. Professor Jun Zhao of Guanghua Law School, Zhejiang University, Assistant Professor Fan Yang of the School of Law, City University of Hong Kong, Attorney-at-Law Basil Bitas of the Bars of New York State and Washington D.C., Associate Professor Chao Wang of Guanghua Law School, Zhejiang University and Mr. Tim Wong, a barrister from Hong Kong, were invited to join the WG at its second meeting. Mr. Daniel Fung prepared and sent his paper to the WG but could not attend the meeting at the last moment due to unexpected circumstances.

The second WG meeting lasted for a day and a half. Members discussed in length papers presented by Professor Hsu, Professor Yi, Professor Sharma and Ambassador Manickham. It was decided that all the paper presenters would revise their papers by taking into account the views expressed at the meeting. Professor Jun Zhao would help in providing information and rules relating to transparency and qualification and code of conduct of arbitrators, and so on. Professor Zhao was also in charge of translating the papers from English into Chinese.

At the second meeting of the WG, it was also decided that after receiving the revised papers, Assistant Professor Fan Yang and Professor Guiguo Wang would compile a draft proposal for consideration by the WG members and then members of the Academy.

The third meeting of the WG was held in June 2016 in Hong Kong, China, with participation of the members of the Academy who gave their views on the draft which proposed rules of dispute resolution for the Belt and Road. With views and comments given by all the participants taken into consideration, this dispute resolution mechanism for the Belt and Road is presented here.

Chapter 2
The Background: Existing Systems

2.1 Three Main Categories of Disputes

The implementation of the Belt and Road Initiative involves trade, investment, IP rights, sanitary and phytosanitary standards, product safety standards, tax laws, competition laws, and so on. It requires the cooperation of governments and the participation of enterprises and individuals along the B&R. The cooperation, on the one hand, needs the relevant countries' coordination at political, legal and administrative levels and, on the other hand, needs to regulate the activities of enterprises and individuals. In such an enormous economic cooperation process of the Belt and Road Initiative, disputes are inevitable. Consequently, how to settle the disputes is in fact an issue that the Belt and Road Initiative must face.

Broadly speaking, disputes related to the Belt and Road Initiative may be divided into those between governments, between enterprises, and between a government and an enterprise. If it is classified by the nature of the underlying transaction, such disputes may be subdivided into commercial disputes, international trade disputes and investment disputes. Traditionally, disputes arising from transactions between enterprises (including those between an enterprise and an individual) are treated as commercial disputes, and those arising from inter-governmental cooperation as disputes between contracting states. The other kind of disputes is called investor-state disputes, which are disputes between a foreign investor and its host government. This kind of disputes is more complicated as an enterprise may have a dispute with the host state regarding tax issues, an administrative action or omission or a judicial decision of the latter. Unless a relevant dispute involves obligations under a treaty, such disputes can only be settled by the local court in the country where the enterprise is located or in a manner permitted by the local laws.

However, where an enterprise–government dispute involves an obligation under the World Trade Organization (WTO) agreements or a free trade agreement and where the enterprise believes that a local government's action or omission violates

© Zhejiang University Press 2020

G. Wang et al., *Dispute Resolution Mechanism for the Belt and Road Initiative*,
https://doi.org/10.1007/978-981-15-1975-8_2

such an obligation, the dispute may either be of a trade nature, or belong to the category of investment disputes. In the case of the former, the enterprise may only seek to have the dispute resolved via the government of its own country, in which no compensation may be paid to the affected enterprise.

If the dispute is of an investment nature and there exits an investment agreement or a free trade agreement between the state where the enterprise is incorporated and the state where that enterprise has the place of business, that is host state, the enterprise, as a foreign investor, may be entitled to the settlement of dispute through arbitration with the host state. Thus, depending on the nature of the dispute, the mechanism and applicable rules for the settlement of such disputes differ. The mechanism for settling the Belt and Road-related disputes should be specifically designed to regulate the conduct of dispute resolution according to the category of economic cooperation and transaction and the nature of the disputes therefrom.

2.2 Methods for Resolving the Three Categories of Disputes

1. General Commercial Disputes

A general commercial dispute is an inter-enterprise dispute related to a commercial transaction. The category of such transactions is wide and may include trade, investment, transfer of technology, intellectual property protection, mergers, acquisitions, and divisions of enterprises, sale and purchase of equipment, assignment of concessions, and so on. The shared characteristic of these disputes is that the subject matters are always regulated by the contract between the parties concerned, which includes a method for dispute resolution and governing laws, and so on. It goes without saying that the parties can always choose a court for resolving their disputes. However, if the parties are from different countries and unwilling to resort to a court of either country to settle their disputes, most likely they will choose arbitration as a means to settle their disputes arising out of their contract.

Commercial arbitration consists of institutional arbitration and *ad hoc* arbitration. In institutional arbitration, the legally registered arbitration institution has a physical office, a secretariat and, usually, its own arbitration rules, and so on. *Ad hoc* arbitration is the practice wherein, after the occurrence of a dispute, the parties concerned organize an *ad hoc* arbitral tribunal according to their contract to settle their disputes.

In practice, not all arbitration institutions have their own arbitration rules. Commercial arbitration has now become a very competitive professional business among different institutions. Every arbitration body tries to provide convenient and effective arbitration rules as well as fair and just awards for the purpose of winning recognition and appreciation of the parties so that they would select it as the arbitration body. However, the fairness and justice of an award is very hard to define and determine, so providing convenient and effective arbitration rules has become a practical method of assessing the competence and standing of an arbitration institution.

Currently, the United Nations Commission on International Trade Law (UNCITRAL) Arbitration Rules are widely accepted. They are not only widely adopted in *ad hoc* arbitrations but also adopted by some arbitration institutions, such as the Hong Kong International Arbitration Centre (HKIAC) and the Permanent Court of Arbitration (PCA), as their own arbitration rules.

Arbitration rules concern arbitration procedure. An arbitral tribunal, when analyzing and adjudicating the rights and obligations of parties under a contract, also needs to refer to substantive law, namely applicable law. In contracts for sale and purchase of goods, many contracting parties select the United Nations Convention on Contracts for the International Sale of Goods (CISG) as the governing law of the contract. This convention has also influenced the development of national legislation on sale of goods.

Another developing trend in international commercial arbitration is that there is ever increasing emphasis on mediation in the arbitration process or as a separate preliminary step of arbitration proceedings. In practice, very often mediation is combined with arbitration, which has triggered different views on whether an arbitrator should be permitted to serve as a mediator in the same dispute, either before the arbitration proceedings or in the middle of arbitration proceedings. Some consider that successful mediation requires the parties concerned to disclose to the mediator the true facts of the dispute as well as their wishes and basic conditions for arriving at a settlement through mediation, including the upper limit of the amount of compensation and the lowest acceptable amount of compensation, and so on. Where mediation fails, such information may impact the award by the arbitral tribunal that has just conducted the mediation. For example, in mediation, a party may make a concession for compromise, but the concession may leave an impression on the arbitral tribunal that the conceding party committed the breach of the contract in question. If mediation fails, the party concerned may be left in an unfavorable position. In addition to the above-mentioned concern, how to ensure enforcement of the mediation agreement is also a very important issue.

Arbitration is a means for resolving disputes. The effectiveness of the arbitral award depends on enforceability of the award. At present, the most influential mechanism for enforcement of an arbitral award is the Convention on the Recognition and Enforcement of Foreign Arbitral Awards of 1958, also known as the New York Convention, which now has 156 contracting parties. According to the New York Convention, all contracting parties have the obligation to recognize and execute foreign arbitral awards made in the other contracting parties. According to the convention, courts of all contracting parties must not carry out a substantive examination of an arbitral award or set aside an arbitral award. Article 5 of the convention specifies several exceptions to the obligation to recognize and enforce arbitral awards. A court of a contracting party, even if it refuses to enforce an arbitral award on the ground that the award falls within any of the exceptions under Article 5, must not set aside the award. It is worth pointing out that it is not easy to establish the existence of an exception specified in Article 5. Therefore, the 1958

New York Convention has been proved to be a considerably effective mechanism for recognition and enforcement of foreign arbitral awards.

2. **Disputes Among the WTO Members**

The WTO has its own dispute resolution mechanism for the settlement of disputes involving trade agreements among members. The WTO's dispute resolution principle is one of the promoting compliances with the WTO commitments. On a member's violation of treaty provisions, the WTO will first require the member to rectify the measures which are not in conformity with treaty obligations, and the member may do so by, for example, revising or repealing the laws, policies or other administrative measures in question.

As long as a member remedies the situation by eliminating the violation of treaty obligations, it is free from any legal responsibility for the alleged breach. If a member who has violated a treaty obligation refuses to bring the measure into compliance as required, the prevailing party, namely the affected WTO member, may be authorized by the WTO to take retaliatory measures.

Retaliatory measures work this way. The affected party may withhold from the party in violation of the WTO obligations, benefits arising out of the WTO agreements, but in accordance with the WTO rules on retaliation. The retaliatory measures are subject to the principle that such action must at first be directed at the same sector of trade or services. If the violation is in the agricultural produce sector, the retaliatory measures should first be directed at agricultural products of the errant member. It is only when the affected member is unable to take retaliatory measures, or it is not practicable to take retaliatory measures, in the agricultural produce sector, that it can suspend benefits of the defaulting party in respect of other products and services. This is called cross-retaliation. It should be noted that the level of suspension of benefits as a retaliation must be proportionate to the nullification or impairment of benefits caused by the impugned measures, and retaliation should be terminated once the member corrects its measures to comply with the WTO agreements.

Only the members of the WTO have standing in the WTO dispute resolution mechanism. Enterprises and individuals of a member cannot bring a complaint against another member and could only persuade their government to make a complaint.

In a case of complaint, the WTO's dispute resolution body will first require the disputing members to resolve the dispute through consultation, and submit their dispute to a panel if consultation fails. The consultation should be held within 30 days after the date of filing of the request for consultation. The requested members should acknowledge the receipt of the request for consultation. If a requested member fails to reply within 10 days after receiving the request for consultation, or both parties fail to carry out consultation within 30 days after the date of the request for consultation, the member requesting consultation can directly request the establishment of a panel. This process is aimed at raising the efficiency of the dispute resolution mechanism, and is mandatory.

The panel members of the WTO dispute resolution body are in general appointed through consultation by the disputing members, failing which the director-general would appoint the panel members. Except in exceptional circumstances, the concerned parties are not expected to object to the appointment of the panel. Theoretically, the panel is only responsible for finding the facts, making a decision and writing a report. In practice, operation of the panel is very similar to a court of the first instance in the common law system. Any of the parties, if dissatisfied with the findings of the panel, can appeal to the appellate tribunal.

The WTO appellate body consists of seven members, who are responsible for hearing the appeal of relevant members on legal issues involved in the panel report. Considering the appellate body only handles legal issues, any factual matter argued and decided at the panel stage must not be put forward in the appeal stage.

The panel's report, if not appealed, or the appellate body's report on appeal, is submitted to the dispute settlement body (DSB) for adoption. The WTO's dispute settlement body adopts the report following the principle of reversed consensus, so all reports submitted will be adopted automatically unless it is rejected unanimously.

Arbitration is also a WTO procedure for dispute resolution, mainly for ruling on the reasonable period for defaulting members to correct the impugned measures, suspension of benefits and whether the level of suspension is equivalent to the level of nullification or impairment suffered by the affected member. In normal situations, the original panel dealing with the case is invited as the arbitration panel. The purpose of this provision is to improve efficiency of arbitration, as the panel which dealt with the dispute is familiar with the circumstances of the case.

3. **Investment Disputes**

An investment dispute is the dispute between a foreign investor and its host country, according to the dispute resolution procedures stipulated in the relevant investment treaty. Previously, developing countries preferred to settle investor-state disputes in courts in the country where the investment is made, that is, host country. With the development of economic globalization, all countries compete for foreign investment, so the use of the host country's court system as the forum for dispute resolution has been gradually abandoned, and third-party arbitration has won support for the settlement of investor-state disputes.

Such treaty provisions had been accepted by some countries before the mid-twentieth century, but it was not until the 1990s that these provisions attracted widespread attention. One of the reasons for that was Argentina's economic crisis causing governments to adopt emergency measures, affecting the interests of investors that ultimately made Argentina the respondent of several dozen of investment arbitration cases. Successful bringing of arbitration cases between the foreign investors and Argentina greatly encouraged many others to put their disputes with the host countries to international arbitration. It is the current practice that bilateral investment agreements and the investment chapters of the free trade agreements authorize investors to submit their disputes with the host countries to international arbitration, and it has become the norm that investors and host countries settle their disputes through arbitration.

Unlike the WTO agreements on trade in goods and services, investment arbitration is not governed by multilateral arrangements. Investors initiate arbitration against states through bilateral investment agreements or other treaties containing investor-state arbitration mechanisms, such as the Energy Charter Treaty and the North American Free Trade Agreement. Such agreements usually stipulate the arbitration institutions to be chosen, conditions for jurisdiction, applicable arbitration rules and applicable laws, and so on. In practice, except for the provisions of the treaty itself, customary international law forms part of the applicable law for resolving investor-state disputes.

With regard to selecting the arbitration institution/rules, most bilateral investment agreements and the investment chapters of free trade agreements offer several choices for investors, including consultation and arbitration: Arbitration being either *ad hoc* arbitration (mostly applicable to the UNCITRAL Arbitration Rules) or institutional arbitration. Institutional arbitration mainly relies on the International Centre for Settlement of Investment Disputes (ICSID) established according to the Convention on the Settlement of Investment Disputes Between States and Nationals of Other States of 1965, also known as the Washington Convention. In practice, cases accepted by ICSID are far more than those by other arbitration institutions.

One characteristic of ICSID is that if one of the parties concerned is not satisfied with the arbitral tribunal's award, it can apply for annulment of the award according to the provisions of the Washington Convention. Deviating from the original intent of the contracting parties, the ICSID's annulment procedure has in recent years become more like an appeal procedure. Perhaps because of this deviation from original intention of the Washington Convention, the annulment procedure has been widely used by both parties to a dispute.

Another characteristic of ICSID is that the Washington Convention stipulates that the contracting parties have an obligation to recognize and enforce the arbitral tribunal's awards. Compared with enforcement of awards of some arbitration institutions or *ad hoc* arbitral tribunals that must rely on the New York Convention, arbitration by ICSID has certain advantages, which is one of the reasons why ICSID has been chosen by most investment treaties for resolving investor-state disputes.

2.3 Difficulties Concerning the Existing Systems

An accurate and comprehensive evaluation of all dispute resolution mechanisms is a near impossible task. Broadly, international commercial arbitration, the WTO's dispute resolution mechanism and investor-state dispute resolution mechanism share the widely known problems of time-consuming processes and high costs. Without doubt, such problems may differ from institution-to-institution and from mechanism-to-mechanism.

With regard to the WTO and investor-state dispute resolution mechanisms, it is generally considered that enforcement of awards is the biggest problem. The WTO has a relatively comprehensive dispute resolution mechanism, but retaliatory measures (to ensure enforcement) must be authorized. In addition, effective retaliation requires support of an economic powerhouse, which is only available to economically strong members. For example, in the US Gambling case, the complainant was authorized to retaliate but had to abandon retaliatory measures in view of the fact that the US could exert pressure in other international organizations or economic cooperation which would have adverse effect on it. There are other cases, though not many, where strong economic powers have refused to comply with their treaty obligations under the WTO system.

Enforcement in investment arbitration is even more difficult. The Washington Convention, in fact, practices a complete self-discipline system for enforcing awards. In other words, it is entirely up to the host country to enforce or not enforce an award, subject, of course, to pressure from the international community.

Needless to say, the biggest problem in investment arbitration is the operation of the arbitral tribunal, which has been criticized mainly for a lack of coordination and the resultant multiplicity of awards on the same subject matter. Different results from different cases are not uncommon. Yet, where relevant international agreement provisions at issue are almost identical and facts are similar, different arbitral tribunals have arrived at inconsistent decisions. Therefore, some consider that an appeal mechanism should be established in investment arbitration for correcting such problems so that a consistent line of decision may follow.

Arbitral tribunals acting as they see fit is another problem in investment dispute resolution. It is impossible for any treaty to make specific provisions on every matter, which gives arbitral tribunals much discretion. The proper exercise of discretion is certainly a function of the arbitral tribunals. Arbitrary interpretation of treaty texts without giving proper consideration to the intent of the contracting parties has become an intractable problem in investment arbitration. The expanded application of the most favored nation clause is such an example.

An investor-state arbitral tribunal deals with actions and omissions of the host government, and may be said to be virtually exercising a de facto power of judicial review. Yet their conduct of arbitration proceedings remains the same with traditional commercial arbitration, which includes the confidentiality of arbitration. This issue has also come to the attention of the international community at large.

Chapter 3
Preparations for a B&R Dispute Resolution Mechanism

3.1 Establishment of the Dispute Resolution Mechanism

Implementation of the Belt and Road Initiative needs a dispute resolution mechanism which is effective and recognized by the international community. The first issue to be dealt with is the choice of a dispute resolution mechanism. Settling disputes through the courts of the countries along the Belt and Road is not the ideal choice, so alternatives must be explored. As per the above discussion, international economic dispute resolution mechanisms can be classified into three basic categories: commercial arbitration, the WTO dispute resolution system and investment arbitration. These mechanisms have their own advantages and disadvantages. Continuing to use such systems means less risk in using established and familiar institutions, but these may or may not be able to play a role in promoting the Belt and Road Initiative. For example, country-to-country trade and investment disputes under the Belt and Road treaties cannot be settled through the WTO mechanism.

Based on the above discussions, the establishment of a new dispute resolution mechanism by countries along the Belt and Road is proposed. In addition to the government-to-government disputes, enterprises and individuals should also be able to have their disputes with the government of those countries resolved through the mechanism. As a "first step", the system should facilitate early, speedy, fair and affordable resolution of merchant/investor grievances in a non-adversarial manner.

This is particularly useful for long-term projects (such as in infrastructure or natural resources development) where continuity of working relationships may be desirable. This system should therefore provide for an early warning system where a dispute with a foreign merchant/investor may arise and allow coordinated actions to address complaints with a view to resolution. Prior to the matter escalating to a legal action, the relevant government agencies, organizations and individuals "may conduct negotiations and conciliate with foreign merchants/investors according to plan approved by their directly superior agencies after they have opinion of the legal representative agency of the government". Any signs of violations of laws by

© Zhejiang University Press 2020

G. Wang et al., *Dispute Resolution Mechanism for the Belt and Road Initiative*,
https://doi.org/10.1007/978-981-15-1975-8_3

the merchant/investor may also be highlighted. This early-warning and early-resolution/coordination system focusing on the non-litigious stage of a dispute offers a great potential for the Belt and Road countries.

Good offices procedures are part of the WTO dispute resolution system and naturally could be a suitable procedure as the first-stage dispute resolution mechanism for the Belt and Road. It is accordingly recommended here as part of the dispute resolution mechanism.

The proposed mechanism should also try to address the defects of the WTO dispute resolution mechanism, one of which is not to allow private enterprises and individuals in trade to participate in dispute resolutions. In addition, many current services and investments are overlapping considerably. If a dispute resolution system is only responsible for trade disputes but not investment disputes, the parties may have to seek different mechanisms for resolving such disputes, which will not only cause multiple lawsuits but also make it difficult to ensure coordination among such mechanisms invariably resulting in inconsistent approaches and decisions.

Under a unified system, trade and investment disputes will be settled following a unified set of rules.

The establishment of a dispute resolution mechanism by the countries along the Belt and Road can also contribute to the consistent interpretation of treaties so as to truly reflect the intent of the treaty parties and provide consistency. Considering the fact that most countries along the Belt and Road are developing countries, the establishment of such an independent dispute resolution mechanism that takes into account developing country issues can also help the developing countries be further integrated into the economic mainstream of the world.

The independent dispute resolution mechanism should have an appeal system. The problems relating to the lack of an appeal mechanism in investment arbitration have been discussed above. In its model investment agreement and position paper on TTIP negotiations, the EU proposed to set up an appellate institution. The China–Australia Free Trade Agreement also specifies that the establishment of an appeal mechanism should be considered in due course. It may be said that the international community now is not entirely imperceptive of the idea for establishing an appeal system, at least, for investment disputes. As the Belt and Road Initiative covers many countries, its dispute resolution mechanism should be highly forward-looking. The establishment of an appeal procedure is not only of practical significance to the Belt and Road Initiative but can also set in motion a global trend.

Needless to say, the establishment of a Belt and Road dispute resolution mechanism should take a bottom-up approach.

In the process, experts from all countries along the Belt and Road should be involved in discussing and proposing the framework, operational procedures, principles and operational rules of the dispute resolution mechanism. Once a proposal is formulated, it can be submitted to the governments of the Belt and Road countries for consideration. After the governments of these countries have considered the proposal, government representatives should gather together to negotiate on specific provisions and reach agreement.

3.2 The Importance of Mediation

As a matter of principle, the Belt and Road dispute resolution mechanism should consider adopting a combination of mediation and arbitration. The international community views mediation as an Eastern value and tradition. In practice, all Eastern judicial and arbitration bodies including the Chinese courts and arbitral tribunals attach great importance to mediation. In some jurisdictions, mediation is a prerequisite to judicial procedures. For example, all civil lawsuits in Hong Kong must be mediated first, and only when it is confirmed that the parties have conducted mediation and the mediation has failed can a civil case be accepted by a Hong Kong court.

Mediation is a product of Eastern culture, but it is Western scholars who have done serious theoretical studies of it. Institutions in Western countries conduct various courses on mediation which has made mediation much more widely known. The Belt and Road Initiative was launched by China and includes a large number of countries influenced by Eastern culture. Therefore, emphasis on mediation in the Belt and Road dispute resolution mechanism is appropriate to reflect this culture.

While stressing on mediation, we should offer users of the system the choice of selecting it. First, in order to secure recognition by and support of the international community, the mediation rules for the Belt and Road should become widely known and win public trust. Currently, only the UNCITRAL Conciliation Rules and UNCITRAL Model Law on International Commercial Conciliation enjoy such a position. Moreover, as China actively participated in the formulation of the UNCITRAL Conciliation Rules, it will "gain everything and lose nothing", if the Belt and Road mediation rules reflect the UNCITRAL Conciliation Rules.

At the operational level, in line with our proposal that the Belt and Road adopt a combination of arbitration and mediation, the rules should clearly distinguish between mediation and arbitration. A mediator must not serve as an arbitrator subsequent to the failure of mediation. On the other hand, an arbitrator must not participate in mediation, if mediation is initiated in the middle of arbitration proceedings. In this way the Belt and Road's mediation mechanism will be able to avoid the present difficulties facing mediation, giving the mediation system a great step forward. It will surely win the support of the international community.

In order to give full operational effect to mediation, mediation rules should stipulate that mediators as well as parties to mediation are bound by a strict confidentiality obligation. The evidence submitted by the parties, the positions of any party and concessions by the parties made in the mediation stage shall not be used as evidence in the arbitration stage.

There is no doubt that mediation should be promoted as the preferred dispute resolution procedure. However, if mediation fails, arbitration is the inevitable choice. The first issue would be what kind of arbitration rules should be applied. Currently, the UNCITRAL Arbitration Rules are widely recognized by parties and enjoy high public trust. These Rules are not only widely applied in *ad hoc* arbitration but also adopted by arbitration institutions such as the Permanent Court of

Arbitration and the Hong Kong International Arbitration Centre as their own arbitration rules. In order to win the widest support of the countries along the Belt and Road, adoption of the UNCITRAL Arbitration Rules is most probably the best choice. Of course, while adopting these Rules for the Belt and Road Initiative, proper adjustments must be made.

3.3 A Transparent Mechanism

To meet the international community's criticism of investment arbitration, the Belt and Road arbitration procedures should emphasize the principle of transparency. The UNCITRAL Rules on Transparency in Treaty-Based Investor-State Arbitration effective as of April 1, 2014 and the UN Convention on Transparency in Treaty-Based Investor-State Arbitration concluded on March 17, 2015 illustrate that the increase of transparency has become a necessary trend in investment dispute resolution. In this aspect the Belt and Road arbitration mechanism should set an example by adopting the principle of transparency in its dispute resolution mechanism. Where countries along the Belt and Road are the first to sign and adopt the above-mentioned documents, their contributions to arbitration and international economic transactions and cooperation will be of immeasurable importance.

The appellate procedures of the Belt and Road should be formulated by studying the WTO appellate body's rules, practice and procedures, the EU's proposed investment court rules and the practice of annulment procedures of ICSID. The rules should aim at correcting the defects of the system of investment arbitration, particularly the arbitrary exercise of discretion by arbitral tribunals, unauthorized expansion of jurisdiction and attaching less importance or insufficient importance to the contracting parties' intent, and so on. The rules should also authorize the Belt and Road appeal tribunal to make decisions mainly on questions of law. Where in a case evidence which could not have been discovered at the initial tribunal hearing has come into light, the appellate body should have the right to verify the relevant facts and evidence in the light of such new evidence.

As discussed above, ineffective implementation of international treaties in relation to trade and investment is an issue that calls for urgent resolution. The Belt and Road Initiative's dispute resolution mechanism should address this issue as a priority. The alternatives include combination of compensation (such as investment arbitration compensation) with retaliation (such as the WTO retaliation mechanism). This alternative, if adopted, may reduce the risks of ineffective implementation of the Belt and Road agreements.

To sum up, formulating an effective dispute resolution mechanism is helpful for the implementation of the Belt and Road Initiative. Formulation of the mechanism should be based on a full consideration and analysis of how existing systems operate, so as to make a common set of rules for trade and investment. These rules should emphasize on combining mediation with arbitration, maintaining a high degree of transparency and respecting the intent of contracting parties, which should serve as the core principles for the dispute resolution mechanism for the Belt and Road Initiative. Meanwhile, there must be a separation of persons in mediation, arbitration and appeal processes: In a particular case these three stages of conflict resolution should be conducted by different experts. By doing so, we will be able to not only highlight characteristics of the Eastern culture but also eliminate the concerns of the international community relating to the inseparability of mediation from arbitration.

Chapter 4
Rules on B&R Dispute Resolution

4.1 Procedure for Grievance/Good Offices Mechanism

Article 1

Initiation of Claim

A party wishing to initiate the use of the good offices procedure of the Belt and Road Dispute Resolution Center (B&R DRC) (the complainant) shall notify the B&R DRC of its complaint by providing the following information in the prescribed form:

1. The name, postal address, e-mail address and country of registration of the complainant (where the complainant is not an individual);
2. An authorized representative within the complainant organization (where the complainant is not an individual) to participate in the procedure;
3. The relevant treaty or treaties, agreements and its provision(s) alleged to have been breached;
4. The legal and the factual basis for the complaint, including the measure(s) or treatment at issue; and
5. The relief or remedy sought.

Article 2

Preliminary Meetings

1. Upon the receipt of the complaint, the B&R DRC shall acknowledge the receipt of it to the complainant within 2 working days. A copy of the complaint shall be dispatched by electronic means to the relevant individual, government department, body or organization as the case may be (the respondent) complained against.
2. Within 3 working days after such acknowledgment, the B&R DRC shall set an appointment for a preliminary meeting with the complainant. Such an

© Zhejiang University Press 2020

G. Wang et al., *Dispute Resolution Mechanism for the Belt and Road Initiative*,
https://doi.org/10.1007/978-981-15-1975-8_4

appointment shall, as far as possible, be set on a date not more than 21 working days from the date of acknowledgment of the complaint.

3. The preliminary meeting shall be held between the B&R DRC and the complainant who shall be invited at this meeting to explain the complaint in detail.
4. The B&R DRC shall, after the preliminary meeting, contact the respondent, to set an appointment for a preliminary meeting with the respondent for the latter to explain his/her/its position, and how he/she/it proposes to deal with the complaint. Such a preliminary meeting shall, as far as possible, be set on a date not more than 21 working days after the date of the preliminary meeting with the complainant.
5. All preliminary meetings may be conducted face-to-face or via electronic means (such as by videoconference).

Article 3

Conveying Response to Complainant

Upon the completion of the preliminary meeting with the respondent, the B&R DRC shall convey the response and any proposal on dealing with the complaint to the complainant within 2 working days.

Article 4

Conclusion of Good Offices Procedure

1. If the complainant is satisfied with the response and any proposal conveyed in Article 3, the matter shall be recorded as such and closed.
2. If the complainant is not satisfied with the response and/or proposal conveyed in Article 3, the B&R DRC shall record this and either:
   (a) Consult the complainant and respondent within 3 working days after recording this, to determine whether they each wish to have a further meeting with the B&R DRC; or
   (b) Recommend within 3 working days that the complainant consider further action under the B&R DRC regulations, upon which the matter shall be closed for purposes of the good offices procedure.

Article 5

Further Meetings

1. In the case of Article 4.2(a), if further meetings between the B&R DRC with the complainant and with the respondent are determined to be required, Articles 2.3, 2.4, 2.5 and 3 shall apply to such further meetings, *mutatis mutandis*.
2. If, after the further respective meetings, the complainant is satisfied with the further response and/or proposal, Article 4.1 shall apply.
3. If, after the further respective meetings, the complainant is not satisfied with the further response and/or proposal, Article 4.2(b) shall apply.

Article 6

Confidentiality

The B&R DRC shall keep confidential all matters conveyed to it by the complainant and the respondent unless both parties jointly agree to the publication of any matter or information arising from their use of the good offices procedure.

4.2 Mediation Rules

Article 1

Scope of Application

1. These Rules apply to as below when the parties have agreed that these Rules shall apply, whether before or after a difference or dispute arises:
   (a) Mediation of investment-related differences or disputes involving investor (s) and state(s);
   (b) Mediation of disputes arising out of or relating to a contractual or other legal relationships; and
   (c) Mediation of disputes or differences arising between states.

2. The parties may agree to exclude or vary any of these Rules at any time. These Rules apply unless otherwise agreed or derogated from by the parties.
3. When any of these Rules is in conflict with a provision of law from which the parties or a party cannot derogate, that provision prevails.

Article 2

Commencement of Mediation

1. A party wishing to initiate mediation under these Rules shall send a written request to mediate to the other party or parties and to the Secretary-General of the B&R DRC.
2. The mediation shall be deemed to have commenced on the date on which the request is registered in the Secretariat of the B&R DRC.
3. The request shall contain:
   (a) A summary of the differences or disputes sufficient to identify the matter giving rise to the request;
   (b) An identification of any treaty, contract or other legal instruments to which the differences or disputes relate;
   (c) The names and contact details of the requesting party and its representative (s); and
   (d) Either a reference to the agreement to mediate or an invitation to the other party or parties to mediate under these Rules.

4. The first meeting of mediation shall be held within one month after the date of the appointment of mediator(s).
5. Mediation under these Rules may take place at any time, regardless of whether court, arbitration or other dispute resolution proceedings have been initiated.

Article 3

Appointment of Mediator(s)

1. There shall be one mediator unless the parties agree that there shall be three mediators. Where there are three mediators, they ought, by default, to act jointly.
2. The parties may designate as a mediator any person who they consider to be suited to assist them in resolving their differences or disputes as below:
   (a) In mediation proceedings with one mediator, the parties shall endeavor to reach an agreement on the name of a sole mediator;
   (b) In mediation proceedings with three mediators, each party appoints one mediator, and the parties shall endeavor to reach an agreement on the name of the third mediator.

3. The parties shall jointly designate the mediator within 21 working days from the date of the request for the mediation. The party or parties concerned shall notify the Secretariat of the B&R DRC of the appointment of each mediator.
4. If the parties have not jointly designated a mediator within 21 working days, then the Secretary-General of the B&R DRC shall appoint the mediator(s) within 14 working days thereafter.

Article 4

Independence and Impartiality of Mediator(s)

1. A mediator shall be impartial and independent.
2. A mediator shall not be a national, as being registered in the roster of mediators, of either party, unless the parties agree otherwise.
3. Prior to accepting an appointment as a mediator, any person under consideration shall provide a signed and dated Statement of Independence and Availability to the Secretariat of the B&R DRC.
4. In the Statement of Independence and Availability, the person under consideration shall:
   (a) Disclose any facts or circumstances that might call into question the mediator's independence or impartiality in the eyes of the parties;
   (b) State the mediator's availability and willingness to conduct the mediation expeditiously and efficiently within the time limit agreed by the parties or, in the absence of such an agreement, within a reasonable time limit following the mediator's appointment.

5. If, during the course of mediation, a mediator becomes aware of any facts or circumstances that might call into question the mediator's independence or

impartiality in the eyes of the parties, the mediator shall disclose those facts or circumstances to the parties in writing without delay.

Article 5

Resignation and Replacement of Mediator(s)

1. If, during the course of the mediation, a party objects for any reason to a mediator continuing to act, then that party shall notify the mediator, the other party and the Secretariat of the B&R DRC. The notification should preferably state the reasons for the objection.
   (a) Any other party to the mediation may comment in writing on the objection within 7 working days after the receipt of the objection.
   (b) Following consideration of the objection and any comment on the objection, the Secretary-General shall consult directly with the objecting party at a meeting or otherwise discuss the objection within 7 working days after the receipt of any comment on the objection, and suggest an appropriate resolution, including the resignation of such a mediator within another 7 working days.

2. If a mediator resigns, is incapacitated or otherwise becomes unable to perform the mediator's functions, a new mediator shall be designated pursuant to these Rules.

Article 6

Role of Mediator(s)

1. The mediator(s) assist(s) the parties in an independent and impartial manner in their attempt to reach an amicable settlement of their dispute.
2. The mediator will be guided by the Code of Conduct for Arbitrators and Mediators, principles of objectivity, fairness and justice, giving consideration to, among other things, the rights and obligations of the parties, the usage of the trade concerned and the circumstances surrounding the dispute, including any previous business practices between the parties.
3. The mediator may conduct the proceedings in such a manner as he considers appropriate, taking into account the circumstances of the case, the wishes the parties may express, including any request by a party that the mediator hear oral statements, and the need for a speedy settlement of the dispute.
4. The mediator shall assist the parties to reach an agreement on a settlement of their dispute on a voluntary basis in which the parties make free, informed and self-determined choices as to the process and the outcome. The parties shall cooperate with the mediator and each other in good faith to advance the mediation as expeditiously and efficiently as possible.
5. With the agreement of the parties, the mediator may consult one or more experts.

Article 7

Representation of the Parties

Each party may be represented or assisted by agents, counsels or advocates whose names shall be notified by that party to the mediator.

Article 8

Language

The parties may agree on the use of one language to be used in the proceeding. If the parties do not agree on any such procedural language, the official language shall be English.

Article 9

Conduct of the Mediation

1. The mediation shall be conducted in accordance with the parties' wishes and with the assistance of the mediator.
2. The mediator may communicate with the parties orally or in writing, together or individually, at any point during the mediation. The mediator may conduct meetings with one party only.
3. No information provided orally by a party to the mediator during a separate meeting may be disclosed to any other party by the mediator, unless the party explicitly authorizes the mediator.
4. In a co-mediation, each co-mediator shall share with the other co-mediator all written or oral communications received from a party or parties. The co-mediators shall coordinate their efforts and jointly conduct the mediation.
5. The mediator may at any time during the proceedings suggest or request that a party provide such additional information or materials as the mediator sees fit.

Article 10

Settlement

1. Each party may, on his/her own initiative or at the invitation of the mediator, submit to the mediator suggestions for the settlement of the dispute.
2. When it appears to the mediator elements of a settlement which would be acceptable to the parties exist, he/she formulates the terms of a possible settlement and submits them to the parties for their observations. After receiving the observations of the parties, the mediator may reformulate the terms of a possible settlement in light of such observations. Yet, the mediator shall not have the authority to impose on the parties any partial or full settlement of the differences or disputes.
3. If the parties reach an agreement on a settlement of the dispute, they draw up and sign a written settlement agreement. If requested by the parties, the mediator draws up, or assists the parties in drawing up, the settlement agreement.

4. By signing the settlement agreement, the parties put an end to the dispute and are legally bound by the agreement.
5. If the parties agree to formalize their settlement in an arbitral award for the purpose of enforcement, the mediator(s) conduct(s) his/her/their mediation in expedited arbitration proceedings, unless the parties agree otherwise.

Article 11

Termination of Mediation Proceedings

1. The proceedings are terminated.
   (a) By signing of the settlement agreement by the parties, on the date of the agreement; or
   (b) By a written declaration of the mediator, after consultation with the parties, to the effect that further efforts at mediation are no longer justified, on the date of the declaration; or
   (c) By a written declaration of one party or the parties addressed to the mediator to the effect that the mediation proceedings are terminated, on the date of the declaration.

2. The declaration of termination shall be made and sent to the Secretariat of the B&R DRC without delay.

Article 12

Resort to Arbitral or Judicial Proceedings

The parties undertake not to initiate, during the mediation proceedings, any arbitral or judicial proceedings in respect of a dispute that is the subject of the mediation proceedings. However, a party may initiate arbitral or judicial proceedings where, in his/her/its opinion, such proceedings are necessary for preserving his/her/its rights.

Article 13

Confidentiality

The mediator and the parties must keep all matters relating to the mediation proceedings confidential. Confidentiality also extends to the settlement agreement, except where its disclosure is necessary for purposes of implementation and enforcement.

Article 14

The Mediator's Role in Other Proceedings

The parties and the mediator undertake that the mediator will not act as an arbitrator or as a representative or counsel of a party in any arbitral or judicial proceedings in respect of a dispute that is the subject of the mediation proceedings. The parties also undertake that they will not present the mediator as a witness in any such proceedings.

Article 15

Admissibility of Evidence in Other Proceedings

The parties undertake not to rely on, or introduce as evidence in arbitral or judicial proceedings, whether or not such proceedings relate to the dispute that is the subject of the mediation proceedings, any of the following:

(a) Views expressed or suggestions made by the other party in respect of a possible settlement of the dispute;
(b) Admissions made by the other party in the course of the mediation proceedings;
(c) Proposals made by the mediator;
(d) The fact that the other party has indicated his/her/its willingness to accept a proposal for settlement made by the mediator.

Article 16

Costs

1. Before the commencement of mediation proceedings, the Secretariat shall provide the parties with the information about the proposed costs. Upon termination of the mediation proceedings, the Secretary-General fixes the costs of the mediation and gives written notice thereof to the parties. The term "costs" includes only:
   (a) The fee of the mediator which shall be reasonable in amount and the travel and other expenses of the mediator;
   (b) The administrative expenses of the B&R DRC;
   (c) The travel and other expenses of witnesses requested by the mediator with the consent of the parties;
   (d) The cost of any expert advice requested by the mediator with the consent of the parties.

2. The costs, as defined above, are borne equally by the parties unless the settlement agreement provides for a different apportionment. All other expenses incurred by a party are borne by that party.
3. The Secretary-General of the B&R RDC may request each party to deposit an equal amount as an advance for the costs and expenses.

4.3 Arbitration Rules

Introductory Rules

Article 1

Scope of Application

1. Where the parties have agreed that disputes between them in respect of a defined legal relationship, whether contractual or not, shall be referred to the Belt and Road Dispute Resolution Center (B&R DRC) for arbitration, then such disputes shall be settled in accordance with these Rules subject to such modification as the parties may agree upon. Such an agreement may be contained in any contract or other agreements in writing prior to the arising of the dispute or may be contained after the dispute has arisen. The parties shall be obligated to respect the agreement to arbitrate and shall not seek to circumvent such an agreement by resort to any court of law except to the extent of seeking enforcement of the obligation to arbitrate.
2. These Rules shall govern the arbitration except where any of these Rules is in conflict with a provision of the law applicable to the arbitration from which the parties cannot derogate. In such a case, that provision shall prevail.
3. These Rules shall apply only to arbitrations on covered disputes.
4. For the purpose of Article 1.3, covered disputes are disputes:
   (a) Between private parties;
   (b) Between a private party/parties and a state party, or a state-owned entity; and
   (c) Between state parties.

5. For the purpose of these Rules, "mediation" refers to mediation under these prescribed Rules.

Article 2

Notice and Calculation of Periods of Time

1. A notice, including a notification, communication or proposal, may be transmitted by any means of communication that provides or allows a record of its transmission.
2. If an address has been designated by a party specifically for this purpose or authorized by the arbitral tribunal, any notice shall be delivered to that party at that address, and if so delivered it shall be deemed to have been received. Delivery by electronic means such as facsimile or e-mail may only be made to an address so designated or authorized.
3. In the absence of such designation or authorization, a notice is:
   (a) Received if it is physically delivered to the addressee; or

(b) Deemed to have been received if it is delivered at the place of business, habitual residence or mailing address of the addressee.

4. If, after reasonable efforts, delivery cannot be effective in accordance with Article 2.2 or 2.3, a notice is deemed to have been received if it is sent to the addressee's last-known place of business, habitual residence or mailing address by registered letter or any other means that provides a record of delivery or of attempted delivery.
5. A notice shall be deemed to have been received on the day it is delivered in accordance with Article 2.2, 2.3 or 2.4, or attempted to be delivered in accordance with Article 2.4. A notice transmitted by electronic means is deemed to have been received on the day it is sent, except that a notice of arbitration so transmitted is only deemed to have been received on the day it reaches the addressee's electronic address.
6. For the purpose of calculating a period of time under these Rules, such a period shall begin to run on the day following the day when a notice is received. If the last day of such a period is an official holiday or a non-business day at the residence or place of business of the addressee, the period is extended until the first business day which follows. Official holidays or non-business days occurring during the running of the period of time are included in calculating the period.
7. The parties shall file with the Secretariat of the B&R DRC a copy of any notice, communication or proposal concerning the arbitral proceedings.
8. Except as provided for in these Rules, the Secretary-General of the B&R DRC may at any time extend or shorten any time limits prescribed under these Rules.

Article 3

Choice of Forum

For the purpose of covered state–state disputes, unless the states have agreed to have exclusive recourse to the B&R DRC, resource to these Rules shall be without prejudice to any action in the WTO framework, including dispute resolution action, or in any other international agreement to which both sates are parties.

Article 4

Notice of Arbitration

1. The party or parties initiating recourse to arbitration (hereinafter called the "claimant") against the other party or parties (hereinafter called the "respondent") shall file a written notice of arbitration to the Secretariat of the B&R DRC.
2. Arbitral proceedings shall be deemed to commence on the date on which the notice of arbitration is received by the Secretariat of the B&R DRC.

3. The notice of arbitration shall include the following:
   (a) A demand that the dispute be referred to arbitration;
   (b) The names and contact details of the parties;
   (c) Identification of the arbitration agreement that is invoked;
   (d) Identification of any contract or other legal instruments and relevant measures out of or in relation to which the dispute arises or, in the absence of such a contract or instrument and a relevant measure, a brief description of the relevant relationship;
   (e) A brief description of the claim and an indication of the amount involved, if any;
   (f) The relief or remedy or declaration sought;
   (g) A proposal as to the number of arbitrators, language and place of arbitration, if the parties have not previously agreed thereon;
   (h) Whether the parties (except the state parties) have attempted to resolve the dispute(s) by using Good Offices and Mediation Rules or mediation under other institutional mediation rules as the case may be.

4. The notice of arbitration may also include:
   (a) A proposal for the appointment of a sole arbitrator referred to in Article 13.1;
   (b) Notification of the appointment of an arbitrator referred to in Article 14 or 15.

5. The constitution of the arbitral tribunal shall not be hindered by any controversy with respect to the sufficiency of the notice of arbitration, which shall be finally resolved by the arbitral tribunal.
6. The claimant shall at the same time send a copy of the notice of arbitration to the respondent, and it shall notify the Secretariat of the B&R DRC that it has done so, specifying the mode of service employed and the date of service.

Article 5

Response to the Notice of Arbitration

1. Within 30 working days after the receipt of the notice of arbitration, the respondent shall communicate to the claimant a response to the notice of arbitration, which shall include:
   (a) The name and contact details of each respondent;
   (b) A response to the information set forth in the notice of arbitration, pursuant to Articles 4.3(c) to 4.3(g);
   (c) A clear and unambiguous response to Article 4.3(h) as to whether parties have used or attempted to use the mandatory process for resolving disputes under the Rules by using Good Offices and Mediation Rules or mediation under other institutional mediation rules as the case may be.

2. The response to the notice of arbitration may also include:
   (a) Any plea that an arbitral tribunal to be constituted under these Rules lacks jurisdiction;
   (b) A proposal for the appointment of a sole arbitrator referred to in Article 13.1;
   (c) Notification of the appointment of an arbitrator referred to in Article 14 or 15;
   (d) A brief description of counterclaims or claims for the purpose of a setoff, if any, including where relevant, an indication of the amounts involved, and the relief or remedy sought;
   (e) A notice of arbitration in accordance with Article 4 in case the respondent formulates a claim against a party to the arbitration agreement other than the claimant.

3. The constitution of the arbitral tribunal shall not be hindered by any controversy with respect to the respondent's failure to communicate a response to the notice of arbitration, or an incomplete or late response to the notice of arbitration, which shall be finally resolved by the arbitral tribunal.
4. The respondent shall at the same time send a copy of the response to the Secretariat of the B&R DRC, and shall notify the Secretariat of B&R DRC the mode of service of the response employed and the date of service.

Article 6

Non-commencement of Arbitration

Recourse to Good Offices and Mediation Rules or mediation under other institutional mediation rules as the case may be for resolution of any dispute is mandatory before commencement of Arbitration under these Rules. Where Good Offices and Mediation Rules or mediation under other institutional mediation rules, as the case may be, have not been exhausted, the Secretariat of the B&R DRC shall advise the parties to use Good Offices and Mediation Rules or mediation under other institutional mediation rules, as the case may be, for the resolution of the disputes. Unless the parties have exhausted recourse to Good Offices and Mediation Rules or mediation under other institutional mediation rules, as the case may be, to resolve the dispute, the arbitration shall not commence.

Article 7

Representation and Assistance

Each party may be represented or assisted by the individuals it chooses. The names and addresses of such individuals must be communicated to all parties and to the arbitral tribunal. Such communication must specify whether the appointment is being made for purposes of representation or assistance. Where an individual is to act as a representative of a party, the arbitral tribunal, on its own initiative or at the request of any party, may at any time require proof of authority granted to the representative in such a form as the arbitral tribunal may determine.

Article 8

Third-Party Funding

1. Where there is third-party funding, the party benefiting from it shall notify (a) such funding, (b) the existence and nature of the funding arrangement, and (c) the name and address of the third-party funder to the other party and to the arbitral tribunal, or where the arbitral tribunal is not established, to the Secretariat of the B&R DRC.
2. Such notification shall be made at the time of submission of a claim, or, where the financing agreement is concluded or the donation or grant is made after the submission of a claim, without delay and as soon as the agreement concluded or the donation or grant is made.
3. When applying rules for security for cost, the arbitral tribunal shall take into account whether there is third-party funding. When deciding on the cost of proceedings, the arbitral tribunal shall take into account whether the requirements as provided for in Articles 8.1 and 8.2 have been respected.
4. The parties agree not to challenge such funding on the basis of champerty or maintenance in any court of law or seek to challenge the enforcement of any award in which the third party was involved in any court of law.

Article 9

Designating and Appointing Authorities

1. The Secretary-General of the B&R DRC shall serve as an appointing authority.
2. In exercising their functions under these Rules, the Secretary-General of the B&R DRC may require from any party and the arbitrators the information they deem necessary and they shall give the parties and, where appropriate, the arbitrators, an opportunity to present their views in any manner they consider appropriate. All such communications to and from the Secretary-General of the B&R DRC shall also be provided by the sender to all other parties.
3. When the Secretary-General of the B&R DRC is requested to appoint an arbitrator pursuant to Article 13, 14, 15 or 20, the party making the request shall send to the Secretary-General of the B&R DRC copies of the notice of arbitration and, if it exists, any response to the notice of arbitration.
4. The Secretary-General of the B&R DRC shall have regard to such considerations as are likely to secure the appointment of an independent and impartial arbitrator and shall take into account the advisability of appointing an arbitrator of a nationality other than the nationalities of the parties and other factors such as regional representation.

Article 10

Expedited Procedure

1. Prior to the full constitution of the tribunal, a party may apply to the Secretary-General of the B&R DRC in writing for the arbitral proceedings to be

conducted in accordance with the expedited procedure under this rule where any of the following criteria is satisfied:

(a) The amount in dispute does not exceed the equivalent amount of US $5,000,000, representing the aggregate of the claim, counterclaim and any set-off defense; or
(b) The parties so agree; or
(c) In cases of exceptional urgency; or
(d) Where perishable goods are involved.

2. When a party has applied to the Secretary-General of the B&R DRC under Article 10.1, and when the Secretary-General of the B&R DRC determines, after considering the views of the parties, that the arbitral proceedings shall be conducted in accordance with the Expedited Procedure, the following procedure shall apply:
   (a) The Secretary-General of the B&R DRC may shorten any time limits under these Rules;
   (b) The case shall be referred to a sole arbitrator, unless the Secretary-General of the B&R DRC determines otherwise;
   (c) The tribunal may, in consultation with the parties, determine if the dispute is to be decided on the basis of documentary evidence only, or if a hearing is required for the examination of any witness and expert witness as well as for any oral argument;
   (d) The award shall be made within three months from the date when the tribunal is constituted unless, in exceptional circumstances, the Secretary-General of the B&R DRC extends the time; and
   (e) The tribunal shall state the reasons upon which the award is based in the summary form, unless the parties have agreed that no reasons are to be given.

3. By agreeing to arbitration under these Rules, the parties agree that, where arbitral proceedings are conducted in accordance with the Expedited Procedure under Article 10, the rules and procedures set forth in Article 10.2 shall apply even in cases where the arbitration agreement contains contrary terms unless the parties agree otherwise.
4. Upon application by a party, and after giving the parties the opportunity to be heard, the tribunal may, having regard to any further information that may subsequently become available, and in consultation with the Secretary-General, order that the arbitral proceedings shall no longer be conducted in accordance with the Expedited Procedure. Where the tribunal decides to grant an application under Article 10.4, the arbitration shall continue to be conducted by the same tribunal that was constituted to conduct the arbitration in accordance with the Expedited Procedure.

Composition of the Arbitral Tribunal

Article 11

Number of Arbitrators

1. If the parties have not previously agreed on the number of arbitrators, and if within 30 working days after the receipt by the respondent of the notice of arbitration the parties have not agreed that there shall be only one arbitrator, three arbitrators shall be appointed.
2. Notwithstanding Article 11.1, if no other parties have responded to a party's proposal to appoint a sole arbitrator within the time limit as provided for in Article 11.1 and the party or parties concerned have failed to appoint a second arbitrator in accordance with Article 14 or 15, the Secretary-General of B&R DRC may, at the request of a party, appoint a sole arbitrator pursuant to the procedure as provided for in Article 13.2, if he/she determines that, in view of the circumstances of the case, this is more appropriate.

Article 12

Appointment of Arbitrators[1]

1. To assist in the selection of arbitrators, the Secretary-General of B&R DRC shall maintain an indicative list of individuals, who are willing and able to serve and possess the qualifications outlined in these Rules, from which arbitrators may be drawn as appropriate. Parties to these Rules may periodically suggest names of individuals (up to five), whether their own nationals or not, for inclusion on the indicative list, providing relevant information relating to the qualifications, and those names shall be added to the list. For each of the individuals on the list, the list shall indicate general and specific areas of experience or expertise of the individuals.
2. Parties to these Rules may replace a member on their indicative list at any time.
3. Parties are free to choose arbitrators either from the indicative list or any individual of their own choice who meets the qualifications set out in these Rules.

Article 13

1. If the parties have agreed that a sole arbitrator is to be appointed and if within 30 working days after the receipt by all other parties of a proposal for the appointment of a sole arbitrator the parties have not reached an agreement thereon, a sole arbitrator shall, at the request of a party, be appointed by the Secretary-General of the B&R DRC.
2. The Secretary-General of the B&R DRC shall appoint the sole arbitrator as promptly as possible. In making the appointment, the Secretary-General of the B&R DRC shall use the following list procedure, unless the parties agree that

[1] Articles 13, 14 and 15 are also about appointment of arbitrators, so their names are omitted.

the list procedure should not be used or unless the Secretary-General of the B&R DRC determines, in his/her discretion, that the use of the list procedure is not appropriate for the case:

(a) The Secretary-General of the B&R DRC shall communicate to each of the parties an identical list containing at least three names;
(b) Within 15 working days following the receipt of this list, each party may return the list to the Secretary-General of the B&R DRC after having deleted the name or names to which it objects and numbered the remaining names in an order of preference;
(c) After the expiration of the above timeframe, the Secretary-General of the B&R DRC shall appoint the sole arbitrator from among the names approved in the lists returned to it and in accordance with the order of preference indicated by the parties;
(d) If, for any reason, the appointment cannot be made according to this procedure, the Secretary-General of the B&R DRC may exercise his discretion in appointing the sole arbitrator.

Article 14

1. If three arbitrators are to be appointed, each party shall appoint one arbitrator. The two arbitrators thus appointed shall choose the third arbitrator who will act as the presiding arbitrator of the arbitral tribunal.
2. If within 30 working days after the receipt of a party's notification of the appointment of an arbitrator, the other party has not notified the first party of the arbitrator it has appointed, the first party may request the Secretary-General of the B&R DRC to appoint the second arbitrator.
3. If within 30 working days after the appointment of the second arbitrator, the two arbitrators have not agreed on the choice of the presiding arbitrator, the presiding arbitrator shall be appointed by the Secretary-General of the B&R DRC in the same way as a sole arbitrator would be appointed under Article 13.

Article 15

1. For the purposes of Article 14.1, where three arbitrators are to be appointed and there are multiple parties as the claimant or as the respondent, unless the parties have agreed to another method of appointment of arbitrators, the multiple parties jointly, whether as the claimant or as the respondent, shall appoint an arbitrator.
2. If the parties have agreed that the arbitral tribunal is to be composed of a number of arbitrators other than one or three, the arbitrators shall be appointed according to the method agreed upon by the parties.
3. In the event of any failure to constitute the arbitral tribunal under these Rules, the Secretary-General of the B&R DRC shall, at the request of any party, constitute the arbitral tribunal and, in so doing, may revoke any appointment already made and appoint or reappoint each of the arbitrators and designate one of them as the presiding arbitrator.

4. Under such circumstances, the arbitration agreement shall be treated for all purposes as a written agreement by the parties for the nomination and appointment of the arbitral tribunal by the Secretary-General of the B&R DRC alone.

Article 16

Qualifications

1. All arbitrators shall:
   (a) Have demonstrated expertise in international law. It is desirable that they have expertise in particular, in international investment law, international trade law and the resolution of disputes arising under international investment or international trade agreements, and where the law applicable to the dispute is a foreign law, the parties shall make their best efforts to choose arbitrators who can reasonably be relied on to apply such a foreign law provided such arbitrators need not be qualified and credentialed to practice law in the country whose foreign law is the governing law of the contract;
   (b) Be chosen strictly on the basis of objectivity, reliability and sound judgment;
   (c) Be independent of, and not affiliated with or take instructions from, any party and not be a member of any government; and
   (d) Comply with the Code of Conduct for Members of the Tribunal, the Appeal Tribunal and Mediators attached as Annex 1 hereto.

2. Parties may agree that at least one arbitrator shall have specific professional qualifications or expertise and/or understanding of local or regional culture and practices.
3. An individual shall not serve as an arbitrator for a dispute if that person has participated in good offices, and mediation.

Article 17

Disclosures by and Challenge of Arbitrators[2]

When a person is approached in connection with his/her possible appointment as an arbitrator, he/she shall disclose any circumstances likely to give rise to justifiable doubts as to his/her impartiality or independence. An arbitrator, from the time of his/her appointment and throughout the arbitral proceedings, shall without delay disclose any such circumstances to the parties and the other arbitrators unless they have already been informed by him/her of these circumstances.

All arbitrators shall be subject to the Code of Conduct for Members of the Tribunal, the Appeal Tribunal and Mediators as Annex 1 hereto.

[2]Articles 18 and 19 are also about disclosure by and challenge of arbitrators, so their names are omitted.

Article 18

1. Any arbitrator may be challenged if circumstances that give rise to justifiable doubts as to the arbitrator's impartiality or independence exist.
2. A party may challenge the arbitrator appointed by it only for reasons of which it becomes aware after the appointment has been made.
3. In the event that an arbitrator fails to act or in the event of the de jure or de facto impossibility of his/her performing his/her functions, the procedure in respect of the challenge of an arbitrator as provided for in Article 19 shall apply.

Article 19

1. A party that intends to challenge an arbitrator shall send notice of its challenge within 15 working days after it has been notified of the appointment of the challenged arbitrator, or within 15 working days after the circumstances mentioned in Articles 17 and 18 became known to that party.
2. The notice of challenge shall be communicated to all other parties, to the arbitrator who is challenged, to the other arbitrators and the Secretary-General of the B&N DRC. The notice of challenge shall state the reasons for the challenge.
3. When an arbitrator has been challenged by a party, all parties may agree to the challenge. The arbitrator may also, after the challenge, withdraw from his/her office. In neither case does this imply acceptance of the validity of the grounds for the challenge.
4. If, within 15 working days from the date of the notice of challenge, all parties do not agree to the challenge or the challenged arbitrator does not withdraw, the party making the challenge may elect to pursue it. In that case, within 30 working days from the date of the notice of challenge, it shall seek a decision on the challenge by the Secretary-General of the B&R DRC.

Article 20

Replacement of an Arbitrator

1. Subject to Article 20.2, in any event where an arbitrator has to be replaced during the course of the arbitral proceedings, a substitute arbitrator shall be appointed or chosen pursuant to the procedure as provided for in Articles 13 to 15 that was applicable to the appointment or choice of the substitute arbitrator. This procedure shall apply even if during the process of appointing the substitute arbitrator a party has failed to exercise its right to appoint or to participate in the appointment.
2. If, at the request of a party, the Secretary-General of the B&R DRC determines that, in view of the exceptional circumstances of the case, it would be justified for the party to be deprived of its right to appoint a substitute arbitrator, the Secretary-General of the B&R DRC may, after giving an opportunity to the parties and the remaining arbitrators to express their views:

(a) Appoint the substitute arbitrator; or
(b) After the closure of the hearings, authorize the other arbitrators to proceed with the arbitration and make any decision or award.

Article 21

Repetition of Hearings in the Event of the Replacement of an Arbitrator

If an arbitrator is replaced, the proceedings shall resume at the stage where the arbitrator who was replaced ceased to perform his/her functions, unless the arbitral tribunal decides otherwise.

Article 22

Exclusion of Liability

Save for intentional wrongdoing, the parties waive, to the fullest extent permitted under the applicable law, any claim against the arbitrators, the Secretary-General of the B&R DRC and any person appointed by the arbitral tribunal based on any act or omission in connection with the arbitration.

Arbitral Proceedings

Article 23

General Provisions

1. Subject to these Rules, the arbitral tribunal may conduct the arbitration in such a manner as it considers appropriate, provided that the parties are treated equally and that each party is given a reasonable opportunity of presenting its case during the proceedings. The arbitral tribunal, in exercising its discretion, shall conduct the proceedings so as to avoid unnecessary delay and increase of expense and to provide a fair and efficient process for resolving the parties' dispute.
2. As soon as practicable after its constitution and after inviting the parties to express their views, the arbitral tribunal shall establish the provisional timetable of the arbitration. The arbitral tribunal may, at any time, after inviting the parties to express their views, extend or abridge any period of time prescribed under these Rules or agreed by the parties. Upon the request of the parties, the arbitral tribunal may also draw up terms of reference.
3. If at an appropriate stage of the proceedings any party so requests, the arbitral tribunal shall hold hearings for the presentation of evidence by witnesses, including expert witnesses, or for oral argument. In the absence of such requests, the arbitral tribunal shall decide whether to hold such hearings or whether the proceedings shall be conducted on the basis of documents and other materials.
4. All communications to the arbitral tribunal by one party shall be communicated by that party to all other parties. Such communications shall be made at the same time, except as otherwise permitted by the arbitral tribunal if it may do so under applicable law.

5. The arbitral tribunal may, at the request of any party, allow one or more third persons to be joined in the arbitration as a party provided such a person is a party to the arbitration agreement or, unless the arbitral tribunal finds, after giving all parties, including the person or persons to be joined, the opportunity to be heard, that joinder should not be permitted because of prejudice to any of those parties. The arbitral tribunal may make a single award or several awards in respect of all parties involved in the arbitration.

Article 24

Place of Arbitration

1. The parties may agree on the seat of the arbitration. Failing such an agreement, the seat of the arbitration shall be determined by the tribunal, having regard to all the circumstances of the case, which decision shall be final and conclusive.
2. The arbitral tribunal may meet at any location it considers appropriate for deliberations. Unless otherwise agreed by the parties, the arbitral tribunal may also meet at any location it considers appropriate for any other purpose, including hearings.
3. The award shall be deemed to have been made at the place of arbitration.

Article 25

Language

1. The language of arbitration shall be English.
2. The arbitral tribunal may order that any documents annexed to the statement of claim or statement of defense, and any supplementary documents or exhibits submitted in the course of the proceedings, delivered in their original language, shall be accompanied by a translation into English.

Article 26

Statement of Claim

1. The claimant shall communicate its statement of claim in writing to the respondent and to each of the arbitrators within a period of time to be determined by the arbitral tribunal. The claimant may elect to treat its notice of arbitration referred to in Article 3 as a statement of claim, provided that the notice of arbitration also complies with the requirements of Articles 26.2 to 26.4.
2. The statement of claim shall include the following particulars:
   (a) The names and contact details of the parties;
   (b) A statement of the facts supporting the claim;
   (c) The points at issue;
   (d) The relief or remedy or declaration sought;
   (e) The legal grounds or arguments supporting the claim.

3. A copy of any contract or other legal instrument or relevant measure out of, or in relation to, which the dispute arises and of the arbitration agreement shall be annexed to the statement of claim.
4. The statement of claim should, as far as possible, be accompanied by all documents and other evidence relied upon by the claimant, or contain references to them.

Article 27

Statement of Defense

1. The respondent shall communicate its statement of defense in writing to the claimant and to each of the arbitrators within a period of time to be determined by the arbitral tribunal. The respondent may elect to treat its response to the notice of arbitration referred to in Article 5 as a statement of defense, provided that the response to the notice of arbitration also complies with the requirements of Article 27.2.
2. The statement of defense shall reply to Articles 27.2(b) to 27.2(e) of the statement of claim. The statement of defense should, as far as possible, be accompanied by all documents and other evidence relied upon by the respondent, or contain references to them.
3. In its statement of defense, or at a later stage in the arbitral proceedings if the arbitral tribunal decides that the delay was justified under the circumstances, the respondent may make a counterclaim or rely on a claim for the purpose of a set-off provided that the arbitral tribunal has jurisdiction over it.
4. The provisions of Articles 26.2 to 26.4 shall apply to a counterclaim, a claim under Article 5.2, and a claim relied on for the purpose of a set-off.

Article 28

Amendments to the Claim or Defense

During the course of the arbitral proceedings, a party may amend or supplement its claim or defense, including a counterclaim or a claim for the purpose of a set-off, unless the arbitral tribunal considers it inappropriate to allow such an amendment or a supplement having regard to the delay in making it or prejudice to other parties or any other circumstance. However, a claim or defense, including a counterclaim or a claim for the purpose of a set-off, may not be amended or supplemented in such a manner that the amended or supplemented claim or defense falls outside the jurisdiction of the arbitral tribunal.

Article 29

Early Dismissal Claims and Defenses

1. A party may apply to the tribunal for the early dismissal of a claim or defense on the basis that:

(a) A claim or defense is manifestly without legal merit; or
(b) A claim or defense is manifestly outside the jurisdiction of the tribunal.

2. An application for the early dismissal of a claim or defense under Article 29.1 shall state in detail the facts and legal basis supporting the application. The party applying for early dismissal shall, at the same time as it files the application with the tribunal, send a copy of the application to the other party, and shall notify the tribunal that it has done so, specifying the mode of service employed and the date of service.
3. The tribunal may, in its discretion, allow the application for the early dismissal of a claim or defense under Article 29.1 to proceed. If the application is allowed to proceed, the tribunal shall, after giving the parties the opportunity to be heard, decide whether to grant, in whole or in part, the application for early dismissal under Article 29.1.
4. If the application is allowed to proceed, the tribunal shall make an order or award on the application, with reasons, which may be in the summary form. The order or award shall be made within 60 working days after the date of filing of the application, unless, in exceptional circumstances, the Secretary-General of the B&R DRC extends the time.

Article 30

Pleas as to the Jurisdiction of the Arbitral Tribunal

1. The arbitral tribunal shall have the power to rule on its own jurisdiction, including any objections with respect to the existence or validity of the arbitration agreement. For that purpose, an arbitration clause that forms part of a contract shall be treated as an agreement independent of the other terms of the contract. A decision by the arbitral tribunal that the contract is null shall not entail automatically the invalidity of the arbitration clause.
2. A plea that the arbitral tribunal does not have jurisdiction shall be raised no later than in the statement of defense or, with respect to a counterclaim or a claim for the purpose of a set-off, in the reply to the counterclaim or to the claim for the purpose of a set-off. A party is not precluded from raising such a plea by the fact that it has appointed, or participated in the appointment of, an arbitrator. A plea that the arbitral tribunal is exceeding the scope of its authority shall be raised as soon as the matter alleged to be beyond the scope of its authority is raised during the arbitral proceedings. The arbitral tribunal may, in either case, admit a later plea if it considers the delay justified.
3. The arbitral tribunal may rule on a plea referred to Article 30.2 either as a preliminary question or in an award on the merits. The arbitral tribunal may continue the arbitral proceedings and make an award, notwithstanding any pending challenge to its jurisdiction before a court.

Article 31

Further Written Statements

The arbitral tribunal shall decide which further written statements, in addition to the statement of claim and the statement of defense, shall be required from the parties or may be presented by them and shall fix the periods of time for communicating such statements.

Article 32

Periods of Time

The periods of time fixed by the arbitral tribunal for the communication of written statements (including the statement of claim and statement of defense) should not exceed 45 working days. However, the arbitral tribunal may extend the time limits if it concludes that an extension is justified.

Article 33

Interim Measures

1. The arbitral tribunal may, at the request of a party, grant interim measures.
2. An interim measure is any temporary measure by which, at any time prior to the issuance of the award by which the dispute is finally decided, the arbitral tribunal orders a party, for example and without limitation, to:
   (a) Maintain or restore the *status quo* pending determination of the dispute;
   (b) Take action that would prevent, or refrain from taking action that is likely to cause, (i) current or imminent harm or (ii) prejudice to the arbitral process itself;
   (c) Provide a means of preserving assets out of which a subsequent award may be satisfied; or
   (d) Preserve evidence that may be relevant and material to the resolution of the dispute.

3. The party requesting an interim measure under Articles 33.2(a) to 33.2(c) shall convince the arbitral tribunal that:
   (a) Harm not adequately reparable by an award of damages is likely to result if the measure is not ordered, and that harm substantially outweighs the harm that is likely to result to the party against whom the measure is directed if the measure is granted; and
   (b) There is a reasonable possibility that the requesting party will succeed on the merits of the claim. The determination on this possibility shall not affect the discretion of the arbitral tribunal in making any subsequent determination.

4. With regard to a request for an interim measure under Article 33.2(d), the requirements in Articles 33.3(a) and 33.3(b) shall apply only to the extent the arbitral tribunal considers appropriate.

5. The arbitral tribunal may modify, suspend or terminate an interim measure it has granted, upon application of any party or, in exceptional circumstances and upon prior notice to the parties, on the arbitral tribunal's own initiative.
6. The arbitral tribunal may require the party requesting an interim measure to provide appropriate security in connection with the measure.
7. The arbitral tribunal may require any party promptly to disclose any material change in the circumstances on the basis of which the interim measure was requested or granted.
8. The party, requesting an interim measure, may be liable for any costs and damages caused by the measure to any party if the arbitral tribunal later determines that, in the circumstances then prevailing, the measure should not have been granted. The arbitral tribunal may award such costs and damages at any point during the proceedings.
9. A request for interim measures addressed by any party to a judicial authority shall not be deemed incompatible with the agreement to arbitrate, or as a waiver of that agreement.

Article 34

Emergency Arbitration

1. A party that needs urgent interim or conservatory measures (emergency measures) that cannot await the constitution of an arbitral tribunal may make an application for such measures pursuant to the Rules hereunder. Any such application shall be accepted only if it is received by the Secretariat of the B&R DRC, prior to the constitution of the arbitral tribunal and irrespective of whether the party making the application has already submitted its request for arbitration.
2. The emergency arbitrator's decision shall take the form of an order. The parties undertake to comply with any order made by the emergency arbitrator.
3. The emergency arbitrator's order shall not bind the arbitral tribunal with respect to any question, issue or dispute determined in the order. The arbitral tribunal may modify, terminate or annul the order or any modification thereto made by the emergency arbitrator.
4. The arbitral tribunal shall decide upon any party's requests or claims related to the emergency arbitrator proceedings, including the reallocation of the costs of such proceedings and any claims arising out of or in connection with the compliance or non-compliance with the order.
5. The rules relating to emergency arbitration are not intended to prevent any party from seeking urgent interim or conservatory measures from a competent judicial authority at any time prior to making an application for such measures, and in appropriate circumstances even thereafter. Any application for such measures from a competent judicial authority shall not be deemed to be an infringement or a waiver of the arbitration agreement. Any such application and any measure taken by the judicial authority must be notified without delay to the Secretariat of the B&R DRC.

6. The application shall be supplied in a number of copies sufficient to provide one copy for each party, plus one for the emergency arbitrator, and one for the Secretariat of the B&R DRC.
7. The application shall contain the following information:
   (a) The name in full, description, address and other contact details of each of the parties;
   (b) The name in full, address and other contact details of any person(s) representing the applicant;
   (c) A description of the circumstances giving rise to the application and of the underlying dispute referred or to be referred to arbitration;
   (d) A statement of the emergency measures sought;
   (e) The reasons why the applicant needs urgent interim or conservatory measures that cannot await the constitution of an arbitral tribunal;
   (f) Any relevant agreement and, in particular, the arbitration agreement, legal instrument and relevant measure in the absence of such contracts or instruments, a brief description of the relevant relationship;
   (g) Any agreement as to the place of the arbitration, the applicable rules of law or the language of the arbitration;
   (h) Any request for arbitration and any other submission in connection with the underlying dispute, which have led the Secretary-General of the B&R DRC by any of the parties to the emergency arbitrator proceedings prior to the making of the application.

   The application may contain such other documents or information as the applicant considers appropriate, or as may contribute to the efficient examination of the application.

8. The application shall be drawn up in the language of the arbitration, that being English.
9. If, and to the extent that the Secretary-General of the B&R DRC considers appropriate, on the basis of the information contained in the application, the rules relating to emergency arbitration, a copy of the application and the documents annexed thereto shall be sent to the responding party. If, and to the extent that the Secretary General of the B&R DRC considers otherwise, the parties shall be informed that the emergency arbitrator proceedings shall not take place with respect to some or all of the parties and a copy of the application shall be sent to them for information.
10. The Secretary-General of the B&R DRC shall terminate the emergency arbitrator proceedings if a request for arbitration has not been received by the Secretary-General of the B&R DRC from the applicant within 10 working days after the Secretary-General's receipt of the application, unless the emergency arbitrator determines that a longer period of time is necessary.
11. The Secretary-General of the B&R DRC shall appoint an emergency arbitrator within as short a time as possible, normally within 2 working days after the receipt of the application.

12. No emergency arbitrator shall be appointed after the composition of the arbitral tribunal. An emergency arbitrator appointed prior thereto shall retain the power to make an order within the time limit permitted under these Rules.
13. Once the emergency arbitrator has been appointed, the Secretary-General of the B&R DRC shall so notify the parties and shall transmit the file to the emergency arbitrator. Thereafter, all written communication from the parties shall be submitted directly to the emergency arbitrator with a copy to the other party and the Secretary-General of the B&R DRC. A copy of any written communication from the emergency arbitrator to the parties shall be submitted to the Secretary-General of the B&R DRC.
14. Every emergency arbitrator shall be and remain impartial and independent of the parties involved in the dispute.
15. Before being appointed, a prospective emergency arbitrator shall sign a statement of acceptance, availability, impartiality and independence. The Secretary-General of the B&R DRC shall provide such a copy of statement to the parties.
16. An emergency arbitrator shall not act as an arbitrator in any arbitration relating to the dispute that gave rise to the application.
17. A challenge against the emergency arbitrator must be made within 3 working days from the receipt by the party making the challenge of the notification of the appointment or within 3 working days from the date when that party was informed of the facts and circumstances on which the challenge is based if the date is subsequent to the receipt of the notification.
18. The challenge shall be decided by the Secretary-General of the B&R DRC after it has afforded an opportunity to the emergency arbitrator and the other party or parties to provide comments in writing within a suitable period of time.
19. The place of arbitration shall be the place of the emergency arbitration. In exceptional circumstances and depending on the situation, the parties, the emergency arbitrator and the Secretary-General of the B&R DRC may agree upon the place of the emergency arbitration being different than the place of arbitration for other purposes including for hearings. Selection of a different place of emergency arbitration shall be without prejudice to the place of arbitration.
20. Any meeting with the emergency arbitrator may be conducted through a meeting in person in any location the emergency arbitrator considers appropriate or by video conference, telephone or similar means of communication.
21. The emergency arbitrator shall establish a procedural timetable for the emergency arbitrator proceedings as soon as possible, normally within 2 working days from the date of appointment.
22. The emergency arbitrator shall conduct the proceedings in the manner in which the emergency arbitrator considers to be appropriate, taking into account the nature and the urgency of the application. In all cases, the emergency arbitrator shall act fairly and impartially and ensure that each party has a reasonable opportunity to present its case.

23. The emergency arbitrator's decision shall take the form of an order.
24. In the order, the emergency arbitrator shall determine whether the application is admissible and whether the emergency arbitrator has jurisdiction to order emergency measures.
25. The order shall be made in writing and shall state the reasons upon which it is based. It shall be dated and signed by the emergency arbitrator.
26. The order shall be made no later than 15 working days from the date on which the emergency arbitrator was appointed. The Secretary-General of the B&R DRC may extend the time limit pursuant to a reasoned request from the emergency arbitrator or on the own initiative of the Secretary-General's of the B&R DRC if the Secretary-General of the B&R DRC decides it is necessary to do so.
27. Within the time limit established pursuant the rules relating to emergency arbitration, the emergency arbitrator shall send the order to the parties, with a copy to the Secretary-General of the B&R DRC, by any of the means of communication that the emergency arbitrator considers will ensure prompt receipt.
28. The order shall cease to be binding on the parties upon:
    (a) The termination of the Secretary-General of the B&R DRC of the emergency arbitrator proceedings;
    (b) The acceptance by the Secretary-General of the B&R DRC of a challenge against the emergency arbitrator;
    (c) The arbitral tribunal's final award, unless the arbitral tribunal expressly decides otherwise; or
    (d) The withdrawal of all claims or the termination of the arbitration before the rendering of a final award.

29. The emergency arbitrator may make the order subject to such conditions as the emergency arbitrator thinks fit, including requiring the provision of appropriate security.
30. Upon a reasoned request by a party made prior to the transmission of the file to the arbitral tribunal, the emergency arbitrator may modify, terminate or annul the order.
31. The applicant shall pay US$25,000 for administrative expenses and for the emergency arbitrator's fees and expenses.
32. The emergency arbitrator's order shall fix the costs of the emergency arbitrator proceedings and decide which of the parties shall bear them or in what proportion they shall be borne by the parties.
33. The costs of the emergency arbitrator proceedings include the administrative expenses, the emergency arbitrator's fees and expenses and the reasonable legal and other costs incurred by the parties for the emergency arbitrator proceedings.
34. In the event that the emergency arbitrator proceedings do not take place or are otherwise terminated prior to the making of an order, the Secretary-General of the B&R DRC shall determine the amount to be reimbursed to the applicant, if any.

Article 35

Evidence

1. Each party shall bear the burden of proving the facts relied on to support its claim or defense.
2. Witnesses, including expert witnesses, who are presented by the parties to testify to the arbitral tribunal on any issue of fact or expertise, may be any individual, notwithstanding that the individual is a party to the arbitration or in any way related to a party. Unless otherwise directed by the arbitral tribunal, statements by witnesses, including expert witnesses, may be presented in writing and signed by them.
3. At any time during the arbitral proceedings the arbitral tribunal may require the parties to produce documents, exhibits or other evidence within such a period of time as the arbitral tribunal shall determine.
4. The arbitral tribunal shall determine the admissibility, relevance, materiality and weight of the evidence offered.

Article 36

Hearings

1. In the event of an oral hearing, the arbitral tribunal shall give the parties adequate advance notice of the date, time and place thereof.
2. Witnesses, including expert witnesses, may be heard under the conditions and examined in the manner set by the arbitral tribunal.
3. Hearings shall be confidential unless the parties agree otherwise. The arbitral tribunal may require the retirement of any witness or witnesses, including expert witnesses, during the testimony of other witnesses. But if a witness, including an expert witness, is a party to the arbitration, he/she shall not, in principle, be asked to retire.
4. The arbitral tribunal may direct that witnesses, including expert witnesses, be examined through means of telecommunication that do not require their physical presence at the hearing (such as through video conference).

Article 37

Experts Appointed by the Arbitral Tribunal

1. After consultation with the parties, the arbitral tribunal may appoint one or more independent experts to report to it, in writing, on specific issues to be determined by the arbitral tribunal. A copy of the expert's terms of reference, established by the arbitral tribunal, shall be communicated to the parties.
2. The expert shall, in principle before accepting the appointment, submit to the arbitral tribunal and to the parties a description of his/her qualifications and a statement of his/her impartiality and independence. Within the time ordered by the arbitral tribunal, the parties shall inform the arbitral tribunal whether they have any objections as to the expert's qualifications, impartiality or independence. The arbitral tribunal shall decide promptly whether to accept any such

objections. After an expert's appointment, a party may object to the expert's qualifications, impartiality or independence only if the objection is for reasons of which the party becomes aware after the appointment has been made. The arbitral tribunal shall decide promptly what, if any, action to take.
3. The parties shall give the expert any relevant information for his/her inspection, or any relevant documents or goods that he/she may require of them. Any dispute between a party and the expert as to the relevance of the required information and documents or goods shall be decided by the arbitral tribunal.
4. Upon the receipt of the expert's report, the arbitral tribunal shall communicate a copy of the report to the parties, who shall be given the opportunity to express, in writing, their opinions on the report. A party shall be entitled to examine any document on which the expert has relied in his/her report.
5. At the request of any party, the expert, after delivery of the report, may be heard at a hearing where the parties shall have the opportunity to be present and to interrogate the expert. At this hearing, any party may present expert witnesses in order to testify on the points at issue. The expert witnesses may be examined through means of telecommunication that do not require their physical presence at the hearing (such as through video conference).
6. Experts shall be subject to the Code of Conduct for Members of the Tribunal, the Appeal Tribunal and Mediators annexed to these Rules.

Article 38

Default

1. If, within the period of time fixed by these Rules or the arbitral tribunal, without showing sufficient cause:
   (a) The claimant has failed to communicate its statement of claim, the arbitral tribunal shall issue an order for the termination of the arbitral proceedings, unless there are remaining matters that may need to be decided and the arbitral tribunal considers it appropriate to do so;
   (b) The respondent has failed to communicate its response to the notice of arbitration or its statement of defense, the arbitral tribunal shall order that the proceedings continue, without treating such failure in itself as an admission of the claimant's allegations, and the provisions of this sub-paragraph also apply to a claimant's failure to submit a defense to a counterclaim or to a claim for the purpose of a set-off.

2. If a party, duly notified under these Rules, fails to appear at a hearing, without showing sufficient cause for such failure, the arbitral tribunal may proceed with the arbitration.
3. If a party, duly invited by the arbitral tribunal to produce documents, exhibits or other evidence, fails to do so within the established period of time, without showing sufficient cause for such failure, the arbitral tribunal may make the award on the evidence before it.

Article 39

Multiple Contracts/Legal Instruments/Measures

1. Where there are disputes arising out of or in connection with more than one contract or legal instrument or covered agreement, the claimant may:
   (a) File a Notice of Arbitration in respect of each arbitration agreement invoked and concurrently submit an application to consolidate the arbitrations pursuant to Article 41.1; or
   (b) File a single Notice of Arbitration in respect of all the arbitration agreements invoked which shall include a statement identifying each contract, legal instrument or covered agreement and arbitration agreement invoked and a description of how the applicable criteria under Article 41. 1 are satisfied, and the claimant shall be deemed to have commenced multiple arbitrations, one in respect of each arbitration agreement invoked, and the Notice of Arbitration under Article 39.1(b) shall be deemed to be an application to consolidate all such arbitrations pursuant to Article 41.1.

2. Where the claimant has filed two or more Notices of Arbitration pursuant to Article 39.1(a), the Secretary-General of the B&R DRC shall accept payment of a single filing fee under these Rules for all the arbitrations sought to be consolidated. Where the Secretary-General rejects the application for consolidation, in whole or in part, the claimant shall be required to make payment of the requisite filing fee under these Rules in respect of each arbitration that has not been consolidated.
3. Where the claimant has filed a single Notice of Arbitration pursuant to Article 39.1(b) and the arbitral tribunal rejects the application for consolidation, in whole or in part, it shall file a Notice of Arbitration in respect of each arbitration that has not been consolidated, and the claimant shall be required to make payment of the requisite filing fee under these Rules in respect of each arbitration that has not been consolidated.

Article 40

Joinder of Additional Parties

1. Prior to the constitution of the arbitral tribunal, a party or non-party to the arbitration may file an application with the registrar for one or more additional parties to be joined in an arbitration pending under these Rules as a claimant or a respondent, provided that any of the following criteria is satisfied:
   (a) The additional party to be joined is *prima facie* bound by the arbitration agreement; or
   (b) All parties, including the additional party to be joined, have consented to the joinder of the additional party.

2. An application for joinder under Article 40.1 shall include:
   (a) The case reference number of the pending arbitration;
   (b) The names, addresses, telephone numbers, facsimile numbers and electronic mail addresses, if known, of all parties, including the additional party to be joined, and their representatives, if any, and any arbitrator who has been nominated or appointed in the pending arbitration;
   (c) Whether the additional party is to be joined as a claimant or a respondent;
   (d) The information specified in Articles 4.3(c) and 4.3(d);
   (e) If the application is being made under Article 40.1(b), identification of the relevant agreement and, where possible, a copy of such agreement; and
   (f) A brief statement of the facts and legal basis supporting the application.

3. The application for joinder is deemed to be complete when all the requirements of Article 40.2 are fulfilled or when the Secretary-General of the B&R DRC determines that there has been substantial compliance with such requirements. The Secretary-General of the B&R DRC shall notify all parties, including the additional party to be joined, when the application for joinder is complete.
4. The party or non-party applying for joinder under Article 40.1 shall, at the same time as it files an application for joinder with the Secretary-General of the B&R DRC, send a copy of the application to all parties, including the additional party to be joined, and shall notify the Secretary-General of the B&R DRC that it has done so, specifying the mode of service employed and the date of service.
5. The Secretary-General of the B&R DRC shall, after considering the views of all parties, including the additional party to be joined, and having regard to the circumstances of the case, decide whether to grant, in whole or in part, any application for joinder under Article 40.1. The Secretary-General's decision to grant an application for joinder under Article 40.5 is without prejudice to the tribunal's power to subsequently decide any question as to its jurisdiction arising from such a decision. The Secretary-General's decision to reject an application for joinder under Article 40.5, in whole or in part, is without prejudice to any party's or non-party's right to apply to the tribunal for joinder pursuant to Article 40.9.
6. Where an application for joinder is granted under Article 40.5, the date of receipt of the complete application for joinder shall be deemed to be the date of commencement of the arbitration in respect of the additional party.
7. Where an application for joinder is granted under Article 40.5, the Secretary-General may revoke the appointment of any arbitrator appointed prior to the decision on joinder. Unless otherwise agreed by all parties, including the additional party joined, Articles 8 to 10 shall apply as appropriate, and the respective timelines thereunder shall run from the date of the receipt of the Secretary-General's decision under Article 40.5.
8. The Secretary-General's decision to revoke the appointment of any arbitrator under Article 40.7 is without prejudice to the validity of any act done or order or award made by the arbitrator before his/her appointment was revoked.

9. After the constitution of the tribunal, a party or non-party to the arbitration may apply to the tribunal for one or more additional parties to be joined in an arbitration pending under these Rules as a claimant or a respondent, provided that any of the following criteria is satisfied:
   (a) The additional party to be joined is *prima facie* bound by the arbitration agreement; or
   (b) All parties, including the additional party to be joined, have consented to the joinder of the additional party.

10. Where appropriate, an application to the tribunal under Article 40.9 may be filed with the Secretariat.
11. Subject to any specific directions of the tribunal, the provisions of Article 40.2 shall apply, *mutatis mutandis*, to an application for joinder under Article 40.9.
12. The tribunal shall, after giving all parties, including the additional party to be joined, the opportunity to be heard and having regard to the circumstances of the case, decide whether to grant, in whole or in part, any application for joinder under Article 40.9. The tribunal's decision to grant an application for joinder under Article 40.12 is without prejudice to its power to subsequently decide any question as to its jurisdiction arising from such a decision.
13. Where an application for joinder is granted under Article 40.12, the date of the receipt by the tribunal or the Secretary-General of the B&R DRC, as the case may be, of the complete application for joinder shall be deemed to be the date of commencement of the arbitration in respect of the additional party.
14. Where an application for joinder is granted under Article 40.5 or Article 40.12, any party who has not nominated an arbitrator or otherwise participated in the constitution of the tribunal shall be deemed to have waived its right to nominate an arbitrator or otherwise participate in the constitution of the tribunal, without prejudice to the right of such a party to challenge an arbitrator pursuant to Articles 18 and 19.
15. Where an application for joinder is granted under Article 40.5 or Article 40.12, the requisite filing fee under these Rules shall be payable for any additional claim or counterclaim.

Article 41

Consolidation

1. If the arbitral tribunal has been established regarding a matter, and another party requests the establishment of an arbitral tribunal regarding the same matter, whenever feasible, the earlier established arbitral tribunal should examine those complaints.

2. Prior to the constitution of any tribunal in the arbitrations sought to be consolidated, a party may file an application with the Secretary-General of the B&R DRC to consolidate two or more arbitrations pending under these Rules into a single arbitration, provided that any of the following criteria is satisfied in respect of the arbitrations to be consolidated:
   (a) All parties have agreed to the consolidation;
   (b) All the claims in the arbitrations are made under the same arbitration agreement, legal instrument or measure; or
   (c) The arbitration agreements are compatible, and: (i) the disputes arise out of the same legal relationship(s), (ii) the disputes arise out of contracts consisting of a principal contract and its ancillary contract(s), or (iii) the disputes arise out of the same transaction or series of transactions.

3. An application for consolidation under Article 41.2 shall include:
   (a) The case reference numbers of the arbitrations sought to be consolidated;
   (b) The names, addresses, telephone numbers, facsimile numbers and electronic mail addresses, if known, of all parties and their representatives, if any, and any arbitrator who has been nominated or appointed in the arbitrations sought to be consolidated;
   (c) The information specified in Articles 4.3(c) and 4.3(d);
   (d) If the application is being made under Article 41.2(a), identification of the relevant agreement, legal instruments or measures and, where possible, a copy of such an agreement, legal instruments or measures; and
   (e) A brief statement of the facts and legal basis supporting the application.

4. The party applying for consolidation under Article 41.2 shall, at the same time as it files an application for consolidation with the Secretary-General of the B&R DRC, send a copy of the application to all parties and shall notify the Secretary-General of the B&R DRC that it has done so, specifying the mode of service employed and the date of service.
5. The Secretary-General shall, after considering the views of all parties, and having regard to the circumstances of the case, decide whether to grant, in whole or in part, any application for consolidation under Article 41.2. The Secretary-General's decision to grant an application for consolidation under Article 41.5 is without prejudice to the tribunal's power to subsequently decide any question as to its jurisdiction arising from such a decision. The Secretary-General's decision to reject an application for consolidation under Article 41.5, in whole or in part, is without prejudice to any party's right to apply to the tribunal for consolidation pursuant to Article 41.8. Any arbitrations that are not consolidated shall continue as separate arbitrations under these Rules.
6. Where the Secretary-General decides to consolidate two or more arbitrations under Article 41.5, the arbitrations shall be consolidated into the arbitration that is deemed by the Secretary-General of the B&R DRC to have commenced first,

unless otherwise agreed by all the parties or the Secretary-General decides otherwise having regard to the circumstances of the case.

7. Where an application for consolidation is granted under Article 41.5, the Secretary-General may revoke the appointment of any arbitrators appointed prior to the decision on consolidation. Unless otherwise agreed by all parties, Articles 18 and 19 shall apply as appropriate, and the respective timelines thereunder shall run from the date of the receipt of the decision under Article 41.5.
8. After the constitution of any tribunal in the arbitrations sought to be consolidated, a party may apply to the tribunal to consolidate two or more arbitrations pending under these Rules into a single arbitration, provided that any of the following criteria is satisfied in respect of the arbitrations to be consolidated:
   (a) All parties have agreed to the consolidation;
   (b) All the claims in the arbitrations are made under the same arbitration agreement, and the same tribunal has been constituted in each of the arbitrations or no tribunal has been constituted in the other arbitration(s); or
   (c) The arbitration agreements are compatible, the same tribunal has been constituted in each of the arbitrations or no tribunal has been constituted in the other arbitration(s), and: (i) the disputes arise out of the same legal relationship(s), (ii) the disputes arise out of contracts consisting of a principal contract and its ancillary contract(s), or (iii) the disputes arise out of the same transaction or series of transactions.

9. Subject to any specific directions of the tribunal, the provisions of Article 41.3 shall apply, *mutatis mutandis*, to an application for consolidation under Article 41.8.
10. The tribunal shall, after giving all parties the opportunity to be heard, and having regard to the circumstances of the case, decide whether to grant, in whole or in part, any application for consolidation under Article 41.8. The tribunal's decision to grant an application for consolidation under Article 41.10 is without prejudice to its power to subsequently decide any question as to its jurisdiction arising from such a decision. Any arbitration that is not consolidated shall continue as a separate arbitration under these Rules.
11. Where an application for consolidation is granted under Article 41.10, the Secretary-General may revoke the appointment of any arbitrator appointed prior to the decision on consolidation.
12. The Secretary-General's decision to revoke the appointment of any arbitrator under Article 41.7 or 41.11 is without prejudice to the validity of any act done or order or award made by the arbitrator before his/her appointment was revoked.
13. Where an application for consolidation is granted under Article 41.5 or 41.10, any party who has not nominated an arbitrator or otherwise participated in the constitution of the tribunal shall be deemed to have waived his/her/its right to nominate an arbitrator or otherwise participate in the constitution of the tribunal, without prejudice to the right of such a party to challenge an arbitrator pursuant to Article 18.

Article 42

Closure of Hearings

1. The arbitral tribunal may inquire of the parties if they have any further proof to offer or witness to be heard or submission to make and, if there are none, it may declare the hearings closed.
2. The arbitral tribunal may, if it considers it necessary owing to exceptional circumstances, decide, on its own initiative or upon application of a party, to reopen the hearings at any time before the award is made.

Article 43

Waiver of Right to Object

A failure by any party to object promptly to any non-compliance with these Rules or with any requirement of the arbitration agreement shall be deemed to be a waiver of the right of such a party to make such an objection, unless such a party can show that, under the circumstances, its failure to object was justified.

The Award

Article 44

Decisions

1. When there is more than one arbitrator, an award or any other decision of the arbitral tribunal may be made either unanimously or by a majority vote of the arbitrators.
2. In the case of questions of procedure, when there is no majority or when the arbitral tribunal so authorizes, the presiding arbitrator may decide alone, subject to revision, if any, by the arbitral tribunal.
3. An award made by the tribunal shall be a final award under these Rules unless an appeal is filed against it under Article 53. In case of such an appeal, the award shall be a provisional award subject to Article 54.

Article 45

Form and Effect of the Award

1. The arbitral tribunal may make separate awards on different issues at different times and shall deliver the award(s) within 6 months counting from the date on which the arbitral tribunal is formed. In case of special circumstances, this time period for completing the arbitral proceedings may be extended by the Secretary-General of the B&R DRC upon justification of the arbitral tribunal.
2. All awards shall be made in writing and shall be final and binding on the parties.
3. The arbitral tribunal shall state the reasons upon which the award is based, unless the parties have agreed that no reason is to be given.
4. An award shall be signed by the arbitrators and it shall contain the date on which the award was made and indicate the place of arbitration. Where there is

more than one arbitrator and any of them fails to sign, the award shall state the reason for the absence of the signature.

5. An award may be made public with the consent of all parties or where and to what extent disclosure is required of a party by legal duty, to protect or pursue a legal right or in relation to legal proceedings before a court or other competent authorities.
6. Copies of the award signed by the arbitrators shall be communicated to the parties by the arbitral tribunal.
7. The tribunal may award simple or compound interest on any sum which is the subject of the arbitration at such rates as the parties may have agreed or, in the absence of such an agreement, as the tribunal determines to be appropriate, in respect of any period which the tribunal determines to be appropriate.
8. In the case of a dispute where a state is a party, any award of damages shall be determined in accordance with generally recognized international principles of valuation and taking into account, inter alia, an equitable balance between the public interest and interest of those affected, the purpose of the measure, and where applicable, the current and past use of the property, the history of its acquisition, the amount of capital invested, depreciation, duration as a going concern of the undertaking, its record of profitability, capital already repatriated, replacement value and other relevant factors. Compensation shall neither include losses which are not actually incurred nor probable or unreal profits. Compensation may be adjusted to reflect aggravating conduct by a claimant or conduct that does not seek to mitigate damages. In establishing the just quantum of damages, the tribunal shall base its decision on a comparison of multiple valuation methods, where appropriate.
9. No punitive or moral damage may be awarded by the tribunal.
10. Where a government measure relating to trade which does not include measures relating to investment is in dispute, the arbitral tribunal in its findings, cannot add to or diminish the rights and obligations of the state which is a party to the dispute as provided for in the relevant treaty in the dispute.

Article 46

Applicable Law and *Amiable Compositeur*

1. The arbitral tribunal shall apply the law designated by the parties as applicable rules to the substance of the dispute. Failing such designation by the parties, the arbitral tribunal shall apply the law which it determines to be appropriate.
2. The arbitral tribunal shall decide as *amiable compositeur* or *ex aequo et bono* only if the parties have expressly authorized the arbitral tribunal to do so.
3. In all cases, the arbitral tribunal shall decide in accordance with the terms of the contract, if any, and shall take into account any usage of trade applicable to the transaction.
4. The arbitral tribunal shall, wherever applicable, interpret the relevant provisions in accordance with customary rules of interpretation of public international law, including those codified in the Vienna Convention on the Law of Treaties.

Article 47

Settlement or Other Grounds for Termination

1. If, before the award is made, the parties agree on a settlement of the dispute, the arbitral tribunal shall either issue an order for the termination of the arbitral proceedings or, if requested by the parties and accepted by the arbitral tribunal, record the settlement in the form of an arbitral award on agreed terms. The arbitral tribunal is not obliged to give reasons for such an award.
2. If, before the award is made, the continuation of the arbitral proceedings becomes unnecessary or impossible for any reason not mentioned in Article 47.1, the arbitral tribunal shall inform the parties of its intention to issue an order for the termination of the proceedings. The arbitral tribunal shall have the power to issue such an order unless there are remaining matters that may need to be decided and the arbitral tribunal considers it appropriate to do so.
3. Copies of the order for termination of the arbitral proceedings or of the arbitral award on agreed terms, signed by the arbitrators, shall be communicated by the arbitral tribunal to the parties and the Secretary-General of B&R DRC. Where an arbitral award on agreed terms is made, the provisions of Article 45.2, 45.4 and 45.5, shall apply.

Article 48

Interpretation of the Award

1. Within 30 working days following the receipt of the award, a party, with notice to the other parties, may request that the arbitral tribunal give an interpretation of the award.
2. The interpretation shall be given in writing within 45 working days following the receipt of the request. The interpretation shall form part of the award and the provisions of Article 45, Paragraphs 2 to 6, shall apply.

Article 49

Correction of the Award

1. Within 30 working days after the receipt of the award, a party, with notice to the other parties, may request the arbitral tribunal to correct in the award any error in computation, any clerical or typographical error, or any error or omission of a similar nature. If the arbitral tribunal considers that the request is justified, it shall make the correction within 45 working days after the receipt of the request.
2. The arbitral tribunal may within 30 working days following the communication of the award make such corrections on its own initiative.
3. Such corrections shall be in writing and shall form part of the award. The provisions of Articles 45.2 to 45.6, shall apply.

Article 50

Additional Award

1. Within 30 working days following the receipt of the termination order or the award, a party, with notice to the other parties, may request the arbitral tribunal to make an award or an additional award as to claims presented in the arbitral proceedings but not decided by the arbitral tribunal.
2. If the arbitral tribunal considers the request for an award or additional award to be justified, it shall render or complete its award within 60 working days following the receipt of the request. The arbitral tribunal may extend, if necessary, the period of time within which it shall make the award.
3. When such an award or additional award is made, the provisions of Articles 45.2 to 45.6, shall apply.

Appeal Procedures

Article 51

Establishment of an Appeal Tribunal and Covered Disputes

1. There shall be a permanent appeal tribunal.
2. These Rules shall apply only to awards of the appeal tribunal on covered disputes.
3. For the purposes of Article 51.2, covered disputes shall not include disputes:
   (a) Between private parties; and
   (b) Between a private party/parties and a state party or state entity which do not arise from a treaty obligation.

Article 52

Composition and Structure of the Appeal Tribunal

1. A permanent appeal tribunal is hereby established to hear appeals from the awards issued by the arbitral tribunal.
2. The appeal tribunal shall be composed of 12 members, of whom eight shall be nationals of those countries that have accepted these Rules (the Belt and Road countries) and four shall be nationals of other countries.
3. The parties, by decision of the Belt and Road countries, shall, upon the entry into force of these Rules, appoint the members of the appeal tribunal. For this purpose, each Belt and Road country shall propose three candidates, two of which may be nationals of that country and one shall be a non-national from a non-Belt and Road country, for the Belt and Road country to thereafter jointly appoint the members.
4. The appeal tribunal members shall be appointed for a six-year term. However, the terms of 6 of the 12 persons appointed immediately after the entry into force of these Rules, to be determined by lot, shall extend to nine years. Vacancies shall be filled as they arise. A person appointed to replace another person whose

term of office has not expired shall hold office for the remainder of the predecessor's term.

5. The members of the appeal tribunal shall possess the qualifications required in their respective countries for appointment to the highest judicial offices, or be jurists of recognized competence. They shall have demonstrated expertise in public international law. It is desirable that they have expertise in international investment law, international trade law and the resolution of disputes arising under international investment or international trade agreements. They shall be unaffiliated with any government.
6. The appeal tribunal shall have a president and a vice president who shall be selected by lot for a two-year term and shall be selected from among the members who are nationals of third states. They shall serve on the basis of a rotation drawn by lot by the Belt and Road countries. The vice president shall replace the president when the president is unavailable.
7. The appeal tribunal shall hear appeals in divisions consisting of three members. The division shall be chaired by the member who is a national of a third state.

Article 53

Scope of Appeal and Appeal Procedure

1. Either party may appeal to the appeal tribunal, within 90 calendar days after the issuance of a provisional award. The grounds for appeal are:
   (a) That the arbitral tribunal has erred in the interpretation or application of the applicable law;
   (b) That the tribunal has manifestly erred in the appreciation of the facts, including the appreciation of relevant domestic law; or
   (c) Those as provided for in Article 52 of the 1965 Convention on the Settlement of Investment Disputes Between States and Nationals of Other States, in so far as they are not covered by Articles 53.1(a) and 53.1(b).

2. The appeal tribunal shall reject the appeal where it finds that the appeal is unfounded. It may also dismiss the appeal on an expedited basis where it is clear that the appeal is manifestly unfounded.
3. If the appeal tribunal finds that the appeal is well founded, the decision of the appeal tribunal shall modify or reverse the legal findings and conclusions in the provisional award in whole or in part. Its decision shall specify precisely how it has modified or reversed the relevant findings and conclusions of the tribunal.
4. An appeal on matters in Article 53.1 shall be carried out on a de novo basis.
5. Where the facts established by the arbitral tribunal so permit, the appeal tribunal shall apply its own legal findings and conclusions to such facts and render a final decision on the matter. Where this is not possible, it shall refer the matter back to the original tribunal.
6. A party lodging an appeal shall provide security, including the costs of appeal, as well as a reasonable amount determined by the appeal tribunal in light of the circumstances of the case.

7. As a general rule, the appeal proceedings shall not exceed 120 calendar days from the date a party to the dispute formally notifies its decision to appeal to the date the appeal tribunal issues its decision. When the appeal tribunal considers that it cannot issue its decision within 120 calendar days, it shall inform the parties in writing of the reasons for the delay together with an estimate of the period within which it will issue its decision. In no case should the proceedings exceed 180 calendar days.
8. The provisions of third party funding, transparency, interim decisions, discontinuance and the non-disputing party shall apply *mutatis mutandis* in respect of the appeal procedure.

Article 54

Final Award

1. A provisional award issued pursuant to this part shall become final if neither party has appealed the award issued by the arbitral tribunal within the time as provided for in Article 53.
2. Where a provisional award has been appealed and the appeal tribunal has rejected or dismissed the appeal, the provisional award shall become final on the date of rejection or dismissal of the appeal by the appeal tribunal.
3. Where a provisional award has been appealed and the appeal tribunal has rendered a final decision on the matter, the provisional award as modified or reversed by the appeal tribunal shall become the final award on the date of the issuance of the final decision of the appeal tribunal.
4. Where a provisional award has been appealed and the appeal tribunal referred the matter or any issue back to the original tribunal, the original tribunal shall, after hearing the parties if appropriate, revise its provisional award to reflect the findings and conclusions of the appeal tribunal. The original tribunal shall be bound by the recommendation and findings made by the appeal tribunal. The original tribunal shall seek to issue its revised award within 90 calendar days after receiving the report of the appeal tribunal. The revised provisional award will become a final award 30 calendar days after its issuance and no further appeal is permitted.
5. For the purposes of this article, the term "final award" shall include any final decision of the appeal tribunal.

Article 55

Working Procedures

The appeal tribunal shall draw up its own working procedures.

Article 56

Decision-Making

1. The appeal tribunal shall hear appeals in divisions in accordance with Article 52.7.
2. A division of the appeal tribunal shall make every effort to reach any decision by consensus. Where, nevertheless, a decision cannot be reached by consensus, a division of the appeal tribunal shall render its decision by a majority of votes of all its members. Opinions expressed by individual members of a division of appeal tribunal shall be anonymous.
3. The decision shall deal with every question submitted to the appeal tribunal, and shall state the reasons upon which it is based.
4. In the interpretation of the agreements/treaties from which the dispute arises, the appeal tribunal shall have regard to its international character and to the need to promote uniformity and certainty in interpretation.
5. The appeal tribunal shall interpret such agreements/treaties in accordance with the Vienna Convention on the Law of Treaties to promote uniformity and certainty.

Article 57

Remuneration

1. The members of the appeal tribunal shall be paid a monthly retainer fee and receive a fee for each day worked as a member, to be determined by decision of the Belt and Road countries.
2. The remuneration of the members shall be paid equally by both parties into an account managed by the Secretary-General of the B&R DRC. In the event that one party fails to pay the retainer fee, the other party may elect to pay. Any such arrears will remain payable, with appropriate interest.
3. Upon a decision by the Belt and Road countries, the retainer fee and the fees for days worked may be permanently transformed into a regular salary. In such an event, the members of the appeal tribunal shall serve on a full-time basis and the Belt and Road countries shall fix their remuneration and related organizational matters. In that event, the members of the appeal tribunal shall not be permitted to engage in any occupation, whether gainful or not, unless exemption is exceptionally granted by the appeal tribunal.
4. The Secretariat of the B&R DRC shall act as secretariat for the appeal tribunal and provide it with appropriate support. The expenses for such support shall be met by the Belt and Road countries equally.

Article 58

Definition of Costs

1. The arbitral tribunal shall fix the costs of arbitration in the final award and, if it deems appropriate, in another decision.

2. The term “costs” includes only:
   (a) The fees of the arbitral tribunal to be stated separately as to each arbitrator and to be fixed by the tribunal itself in accordance with Article 59;
   (b) The reasonable travel and other expenses incurred by the arbitrators;
   (c) The reasonable costs of expert advice and of other assistance required by the arbitral tribunal;
   (d) The reasonable travel and other expenses of witnesses to the extent such expenses are approved by the arbitral tribunal;
   (e) The legal and other costs incurred by the parties in relation to the arbitration to the extent that the arbitral tribunal determines that the amount of such costs is reasonable.

3. In relation to interpretation, correction or completion of any award under Articles 48 to 50, the arbitral tribunal may charge the costs referred to in Articles 58.2(b) to 58.2(e), but no additional fees.

Article 59

Fees and Expenses of Arbitrators

1. The fees and expenses of the arbitrators shall be reasonable in amount, taking into account the amount in dispute, the complexity of the subject matter, the time spent by the arbitrators and any other relevant circumstance of the case.
2. In fixing its fees, the arbitral tribunal shall take the schedule or method of the B&R DRC in determining fees for arbitrators into account to the extent that it considers appropriate in the circumstances of the case.
3. Promptly after its constitution, the arbitral tribunal shall inform the parties as to how it proposes to determine its fees and expenses, including any rate it intends to apply. Within 15 working days after receiving that proposal, any party may refer the proposal to the Secretary-General of the B&R DRC for review. If, within 45 working days after the receipt of such a referral, the Secretary-General of the B&R DRC finds that the proposal of the arbitral tribunal is inconsistent with Article 59.1, he/she shall make any necessary adjustment thereto, which shall be binding upon the arbitral tribunal.
4. (a) When informing the parties of the arbitrators’ fees and expenses that have been fixed pursuant to Article 58.2(a) and 58.2(b), the arbitral tribunal shall also explain the manner in which the corresponding amounts have been calculated;
   (b) Within 15 working days after receiving the arbitral tribunal’s determination of fees and expenses, any party may refer for review such determination to the Secretary-General of the B&R DRC;
   (c) If the Secretary-General of the B&R DRC finds that the arbitral tribunal’s determination is inconsistent with the arbitral tribunal’s proposal (and any adjustment thereto) under Article 59.3 or is otherwise manifestly excessive, it shall, within 45 calendar days after receiving such a referral, make any

adjustment to the arbitral tribunal's determination that are necessary to satisfy the criteria in Article 59.1 of this article. Any such adjustment shall be binding upon the arbitral tribunal;

(d) Any such adjustment shall either be included by the arbitral tribunal in its award or, if the award has already been issued, be implemented in a correction to the award, to which the procedure of Article 49.3 shall apply.

5. Throughout the procedure under Articles 59.3 and 59.4, the arbitral tribunal shall proceed with the arbitration, in accordance with Article 23.1.
6. A referral Article 59.4 shall not affect any determination in the award other than the arbitral tribunal's fees and expenses, nor shall it delay the recognition and enforcement of all parts of the award other than those relating to the determination of the arbitral tribunal's fees and expenses.

Article 60

Allocation of Costs

1. The costs of the arbitration shall in principle be borne by the unsuccessful party or parties. However, the arbitral tribunal may apportion each of such costs between the parties if it determines that apportionment is reasonable, taking into account the circumstances of the case.
2. The arbitral tribunal shall in the final award or, if it deems appropriate, in any other award, determine any amount that a party may have to pay to another party as a result of the decision on allocation of costs.

Article 61

Deposit of Costs

1. The arbitral tribunal, on its establishment, may request the parties to deposit an equal amount as an advance for the costs referred to in Articles 58.2(a) to 58.2(c).
2. During the course of the arbitral proceedings, the arbitral tribunal may request supplementary deposits from the parties.
3. The arbitral tribunal shall fix the amount of any deposits or supplementary deposits only after consultation with the Secretary-General of the B&R DRC, who may make any comments to the arbitral tribunal that it deems appropriate concerning the amount of such deposits and supplementary deposits.
4. If the required deposits are not paid in full within 30 calendar days after the receipt of the request, the arbitral tribunal shall so inform the parties in order that one or more of them may make the required payment. If such payment is not made, the arbitral tribunal may order the suspension or termination of the arbitral proceedings.
5. After a termination order or final award has been made, the arbitral tribunal shall render an accounting to the parties of the deposits received and return any unexpended balance to the parties.

Implementation of Award

Article 62

Non-state-to-state Award

1. By agreeing to arbitration under these Rules, the parties undertake to carry out the final award immediately and without delay, and the parties further agree that any such award shall be final and binding on the parties from the date it is made.
2. Any award resulting out of disputes between private parties, between a private party/parties and a state party, or a state-owned entity may be enforced in accordance with the Convention on Recognition and Enforcement of Foreign Arbitral Awards.
3. Where a measure is in dispute, the parties recognize the importance of prompt compliance and determination finally made by the arbitral tribunal or the appeal tribunal as the case may be (the final award) in achieving the aim of the dispute resolution of the B&R DRC which is to secure a positive solution to disputes.
4. A dispute that is submitted to arbitration under these Rules shall be considered to arise out of a commercial relationship or transactions for the purposes of Article I of the Convention on Recognition and Enforcement of Foreign Arbitral Awards.
5. In case of undue delay the financial costs related to the delayed payment shall be borne by the losing party from the day on which the payment becomes due till the date of actual payment. Such financial costs shall be calculated in accordance with international banking practice.
6. The financial costs of delay do not apply during the pendency of appeal procedure.

Article 63

Implementation of Final Award on a Measure in the Dispute Between States

These provisions are applicable to disputes between states but shall not apply to disputes between states relating to investment agreements.

1. Unless the parties agree otherwise, the responding party shall have a reasonable period of time to eliminate the non-conformity or nullification or impairment if it is not practicable to do so immediately.
2. Particular attention should be paid to matters affecting the interests of developing countries along the Belt and Road with respect to measures which have been subject to dispute resolution.
3. If it is impracticable for the responding party to immediately comply with the final award, the parties shall endeavor to agree, on their own or with the help of a mediator, a reasonable period of time by which the responding party shall implement the final award. If the parties fail to agree on such a reasonable period of time, on their own or with the help of a mediator, within a period of 45 calendar days after the presentation of the final award, any party may, no later than 60 calendar days after the presentation of the final award, refer the matter to

the original arbitral tribunal or the appeal tribunal as the case may be to determine the reasonable period of time through arbitration.
4. The original arbitral tribunal or the appeal tribunal shall take into consideration as a guideline that the reasonable timeframe should not exceed 12 months from the presentation of the final award. However, that time may be shorter or longer, depending on the particular circumstances.
5. The original arbitral tribunal or the appeal tribunal shall determine the reasonable period of time no later than 90 calendar days after the date of referral to the original arbitral tribunal or the appeal tribunal.

Article 64

Non-implementation—Compensation and Suspension of Benefits

These provisions are applicable to disputes between states but shall not apply to disputes between states relating to investment agreements.

1. Compensation and the suspension of concessions or other obligations are temporary measures available in the event that the rulings in the final award are not implemented within a reasonable timeframe. However, neither compensation nor the suspension of concessions or other obligations is preferred to full implementation of a recommendation to bring a measure into conformity with the agreements. Compensation is voluntary and, if granted, shall be consistent with the agreements.
2. The responding party shall, if requested by the complaining party or parties, enter into negotiations with the complaining party or parties no later than 15 working days after the receipt of that request, with a view to developing mutually acceptable compensation, if:
   (a) The responding party has notified the complaining party or parties that it does not intend to eliminate the non-conformity or the nullification or impairment; or
   (b) Following the expiry of the reasonable period of time, there is disagreement between the parties as to whether the responding party has eliminated the non-conformity or the nullification or impairment.

3. A complaining party may suspend benefits in accordance with relevant treaty provisions if that complaining party and the responding party have:
   (a) Been unable to agree on compensation within a period of 30 calendar days after the period for negotiation or mediation on compensation has begun; or
   (b) Agreed on compensation but the relevant complaining party considers that the responding party has failed to observe the terms of the agreement.

4. A complaining party may, at any time after the conditions set out in Article 64.3 are met in relation to that complaining party, provide the written notice to the responding party that it intends to suspend benefits in accordance with relevant treaty provisions of equivalent effect. The notice shall specify the level of benefits that the party proposes to suspend. The complaining party may begin

suspending benefits 30 calendar days after the later of the date on which it provides notice under Article 64.4 or the date that the arbitral tribunal issues its determination under Article 64.5, as the case may be.

5. In considering which benefits to suspend under Article 64.4, the complaining party shall apply the following principles and procedures:
   (a) It should first seek to suspend benefits in the same subject matter as that in which the arbitral tribunal has determined non-conformity or nullification or impairment to exist;
   (b) If it considers that it is not practicable or effective to suspend benefits in the same subject matter, and that the circumstances are serious enough, it may suspend benefits in a different subject matter. In the written notice of suspension of benefits referred to in Article 64.4, the complaining party shall indicate the reasons on which its decision to suspend benefits in a different subject matter is based; and
   (c) In applying the principles set out in Articles 64.5(a) and 64.5(b), it shall take into account:
      i. The trade in the good, the supply of the service or other subject matters in relation to which the arbitral tribunal or appeal tribunal, as the case may be, has found the non-conformity or nullification or impairment, and the importance of that trade to the complaining party; and
      ii. The broader economic elements related to the nullification or impairment and the broader economic consequences of the suspension of benefits.

6. If the responding party considers that:
   (a) The level of benefits proposed to be suspended is manifestly excessive or the complaining party has failed to follow the principles and procedures set out for suspension of benefits in Article 64.4; or
   (b) It has eliminated the non-conformity or the nullification or impairment that the arbitral tribunal or the appeal tribunal, as the case may be, has determined to exist.

   It may, within 30 calendar days of the date after delivery of the written notice for suspension of benefits provided by the complaining party under Article 64.3, request that the original arbitral tribunal (or appeal tribunal) be reconvened to consider the matter. The responding party shall deliver its request in writing to the complaining party. The tribunal or appeal tribunal shall reconvene as soon as possible after the date of delivery of the request and shall present its determination to the parties no later than 90 calendar days after it reconvenes to review a request under Article 64.6(a) or 64.6(b), or 120 calendar days after it reconvenes for a request under Articles 64.6(a) and 64.6(b). If the tribunal or appeal tribunal determines that the level of benefits the complaining party proposes to suspend is manifestly excessive, it shall determine the level of benefits it considers to be of equivalent effect.

7. Unless the tribunal or appeal tribunal has determined that the responding party has eliminated the non-conformity or the nullification or impairment, the complaining party may suspend benefits up to the level the tribunal or appeal tribunal has determined or, if the tribunal or appeal tribunal has not determined the level, the level the complaining party has proposed to suspend. If the tribunal determines that the complaining party has not followed the principles and procedures, the tribunal or appeal tribunal shall set out in its determination the extent to which the complaining party may suspend benefits and in which subject matter in order to ensure full compliance with the principles and procedures set out for suspension of benefits. The complaining party may suspend benefits only in a manner consistent with the determination of the tribunal or appeal tribunal.

Article 65

Compliance Review

These provisions are applicable to disputes between states but shall not apply to disputes between states relating to investment agreements.

1. Without prejudice to the procedures for Non-Implementation—Compensation and Suspension of Benefits, if a responding party considers that it has eliminated the non-conformity or the nullification or impairment found by the arbitral tribunal or the appeal tribunal as the case may be, it may refer the matter to the arbitral tribunal or the appeal tribunal as the case may be, by providing a written notice to the complaining party or parties. The arbitral tribunal or the appeal tribunal as the case may be shall issue its report on the matter no later than 90 calendar days after the responding party provides a written notice.
2. If the arbitral tribunal or the appeal tribunal as the case determines that the responding party has eliminated the non-conformity or the nullification or impairment, the complaining party or parties shall promptly reinstate any benefits suspended under Non-Implementation—Compensation and Suspension of Benefits.

Annex 1
Code of Conduct for Members of the Tribunal, the Appeal Tribunal and Mediators

Article 1

Definitions

In this Code of Conduct:

"Member" means an arbitrator of the tribunal or a member of the appeal tribunal;
"Mediator" means a person who conducts mediation;
"Candidate" means an individual who is under consideration for selection as a member of the tribunal or appeal tribunal;
"Assistant" means a person who, under the terms of appointment of a member, assists the member in his/her research or supports him/her in his/her duties;
"Staff", in respect of a member, means persons under the direction and control of the member, other than assistants;
"Party" means a disputing party.

Article 2

General Ethics

The arbitrators of the tribunal and the members of the appeal tribunal shall be chosen from persons whose independence is beyond doubt. They shall not be affiliated with any government. They shall not take instructions from any government or organization with regard to matters related to the dispute. They shall not participate in the consideration of any disputes that would create a direct or indirect conflict of interest. In so doing they shall comply with this Code of Conduct. In addition, upon appointment, they shall refrain from acting as counsel or as party-appointed expert or witness in any pending or new dispute under this or any other agreement or domestic law.

© Zhejiang University Press 2020

G. Wang et al., *Dispute Resolution Mechanism for the Belt and Road Initiative*,
https://doi.org/10.1007/978-981-15-1975-8

Article 3

Responsibilities to the Process

Candidates and members shall avoid impropriety and the appearance of impropriety, shall be independent and impartial, shall avoid direct and indirect conflicts of interest and shall observe high standards of conduct so that the integrity and impartiality of the dispute resolution mechanism is preserved.

Article 4

Disclosure Obligations

1. Prior to their appointment, candidates shall disclose any past and present interest, relationship or matter that is likely to affect their independence or impartiality or that might reasonably create an appearance of impropriety or bias in the proceeding. To this end, candidates shall make all reasonable efforts to become aware of any such interests, relationships or matters.
2. Members shall communicate matters concerning actual or potential violations of this Code of Conduct in writing to the parties.
3. Members shall, at all times, continue to make all efforts to become aware of any interests, relationships or matters referred to in Article 4.1. Members shall disclose such interests, relationships or matters by informing the parties as soon as possible.

Article 5

Duties of Members

1. Members shall perform their duties thoroughly and expeditiously throughout the course of the proceeding and shall do so with fairness and diligence.
2. Members shall consider only those issues that are raised in the proceeding and are necessary for a decision or award and shall not delegate this duty to any other person.
3. Members shall take all appropriate steps to ensure that their assistants and staff are aware of, and comply with, this Code of Conduct where appropriate.
4. Members shall not engage in ex parte contacts concerning the proceeding.

Article 6

Independence and Impartiality of Members

1. Members must be independent and impartial and avoid creating an appearance of bias or impropriety and shall not be influenced by self-interest, outside pressure, political considerations, public clamor, loyalty to a party or fear of criticism.

2. Members shall not, directly or indirectly, incur any obligation or accept any benefit that would in any way interfere or appear to interfere, with the proper performance of their duties.
3. Members may not use their position to advance any personal or private interests and shall avoid actions that may create the impression that they are in a position to be influenced by others.
4. Members may not allow financial, business, professional, family or social relationships or responsibilities to influence their conduct or judgment.
5. Members must avoid entering into any relationship or acquiring any financial interest that is likely to affect their impartiality or that might reasonably create an appearance of impropriety or bias.

Article 7

Obligations of Former Members

All former members must avoid actions that may create the appearance that they were biased in carrying out their duties or derived advantage from the decisions or awards of the tribunal or appeal tribunal.

Article 8

Confidentiality

1. No member or former member shall at any time disclose or use any non-public information concerning a proceeding or acquired during a proceeding, except for the purposes of the proceeding, and shall not, in any case, disclose or use any such information to gain personal advantages or advantages for others or to adversely affect the interest of others.
2. No member shall disclose a decision or award or parts thereof prior to its publication in accordance with the Rules on Transparency as applicable.
3. No member or former member shall at any time disclose the deliberations of the tribunal or appeal tribunal, or any member's views, whatever they may be.

Article 9

Expenses

Each member shall keep a record and render a final account of the time devoted to the procedure and of the expenses incurred, as well as the time and expenses of his/her assistant and staff.

Article 10

Mediators

The rules set out in this Code of Conduct as applying to members or former members shall apply, *mutatis mutandis*, to mediators.

Annex 2
The Rules on Transparency

Article 1

Applicability of the Rules

1. The Rules on Transparency shall apply to investor-state arbitrations, state-to-state dispute, including appeal process.
2. Exception to the Rules on Transparency is equally applicable to mediation *mutatis mutandis*.

Article 2

Publication of Information at the Commencement of Arbitral Proceedings

Once the notice of arbitration has been received by the respondent, each of the parties shall promptly communicate a copy of the notice of arbitration to the B&R DRC. Upon the receipt of the notice of arbitration from the respondent, or upon the receipt of the notice of arbitration and a record of its transmission to the respondent, unless the Secretary-General of the B&R DRC finds that the dispute is manifestly outside the jurisdiction of the B&R DRC, the B&R DRC shall promptly make available to the public information regarding the name of the parties, the economic sector involved and the treaty under which the claim is being made.

Article 3

Publication of Documents

1. Subject to exceptions to transparency, the state party may, as it considers appropriate, ensure public availability of all tribunal documents.
2. An award may be made public with the consent of all parties or to the extent disclosure is required of a party by legal duty, to protect or pursue a legal right or in relation to legal proceedings before a court or other competent authority.

© Zhejiang University Press 2020
G. Wang et al., *Dispute Resolution Mechanism for the Belt and Road Initiative*,
https://doi.org/10.1007/978-981-15-1975-8

Article 4

Hearings

1. Subject to Articles 4.2 and 4.3, hearings for the presentation of evidence or for oral argument (hearings) shall be public, unless otherwise decided by the arbitral tribunal, after consultation with the parties.
2. Where there is a need to protect confidential information or the integrity of the arbitral process pursuant to exceptions to transparency, the arbitral tribunal shall make arrangements to hold in private that part of the hearing requiring such protection.
3. The arbitral tribunal shall make logistical arrangements to facilitate the public access to hearings (including where appropriate by organizing attendance through video links or such other means as it deems appropriate). However, the arbitral tribunal may, after consultation with the parties, decide to hold all or part of the hearings in private where this becomes necessary for logistical reasons, such as when the circumstances render any original arrangement for public access to a hearing infeasible.

Article 5

Exceptions to Transparency

1. Confidential or protected information, as defined in Article 5.2 as identified pursuant to the arrangements referred to in Articles 5.3 and 5.4, shall not be made available to the public pursuant to Articles 2 to 6.
2. Confidential or protected information consists of:

   (a) Confidential business information;
   (b) Information that is protected against being made available to the public under the treaty;
   (c) Information that is protected against being made available to the public, in the case of the information of the respondent state, under the law of the respondent state, and in the case of other information, under any law or rules determined by the arbitral tribunal to be applicable to the disclosure of such information; or
   (d) Information the disclosure of which would impede law enforcement.

3. The arbitral tribunal, after consultation with the parties, shall make arrangements to prevent any confidential or protected information from being made available to the public, including by putting in place, as appropriate:

   (a) Time limits in which a party, non-disputing party to the treaty or third person, shall give notice that it seeks protection for such information in documents;

(b) Procedures for the prompt designation and redaction of the particular confidential or protected information in such documents; and
(c) Procedures for holding hearings in private to the extent required by Article 4.2.

Any determination as to whether information is confidential or protected shall be made by the arbitral tribunal after consultation with the parties.

4. The tribunal shall decide any objection regarding the designation of information claimed to be protected information. If the tribunal determines that such information was not properly designated, the party that submitted the information may withdraw all or part of its submission containing such information, or agree to resubmit complete and redacted documents with corrected designations in accordance with the tribunal's determination. In either case, the other party shall, whenever necessary, resubmit complete and redacted documents which either remove the information withdrawn by the party that first submitted the information or redesignate the information consistent with the designation of the party that first submitted the information.
5. Nothing in these Rules requires a respondent state to make available to the public information the disclosure of which it considers to be contrary to its essential security interests, or to be contrary to domestic law.
6. Information shall not be made available to the public where the information, if made available to the public, would jeopardize the integrity of the arbitral process as determined pursuant to Paragraph 7.
7. The arbitral tribunal may, on its own initiative or upon the application of a party, after consultation with the parties where practicable, take appropriate measures to restrain or delay the publication of information where such publication would jeopardize the integrity of the arbitral process because it could hamper the collection or production of evidence, leading to the intimidation of witnesses, lawyers acting for parties or members of the arbitral tribunal, or in comparably exceptional circumstances.

Article 6

Submission by a Third Person

1. After consultation with the parties, the arbitral tribunal may allow a person that is not a party, and not a non-disputing party to the treaty (third person), to file a written submission with the arbitral tribunal regarding a matter within the scope of the dispute.
2. A third person wishing to make a submission shall apply to the arbitral tribunal, and shall, in a concise written statement, which is in a language of the arbitration and complies with any page limits set by the arbitral tribunal:

(a) Describe the third person, including, where relevant, its membership and legal status (e.g. trade association or other non-governmental organization), its general objectives, the nature of its activities and any parent organization (including any organization that directly or indirectly controls the third person);
(b) Disclose any connection, direct or indirect, which the third person has with any party;
(c) Provide information on any government, person or organization that has offered to the third person (i) any financial or other assistance in preparing the submission, or (ii) substantial assistance in the two years preceding the application by the third person under this article (e.g. funding around 20% of its overall operations annually);
(d) Describe the nature of the interest that the third person has in the arbitration; and
(e) Identify the specific issues of fact or law in the arbitration that the third person wishes to address in its written submission.

3. In determining whether to allow such a submission, the arbitral tribunal shall take into consideration, among other factors it determines to be relevant:

(a) Whether the submission is within the scope of this dispute;
(b) Whether the third person has a significant interest in the arbitral proceedings; and
(c) The extent to which the submission would assist the arbitral tribunal in the determination of a factual or legal issue related to the arbitral proceedings by bringing a perspective, particular knowledge or insight that is different from that of the parties.

4. The submission filed by the third person shall:

(a) Be dated and signed by the person filing the submission on behalf of the third person;
(b) Be concise, and in no case longer than as authorized by the arbitral tribunal;
(c) Set out a precise statement of the third person's position on issues; and
(d) Address only matters within the scope of the dispute.

5. The arbitral tribunal shall ensure that no submission may disrupt or unduly burden the arbitral proceedings, or unfairly prejudice any party. The arbitral tribunal using such submission may delete the name of the third person.
6. The arbitral tribunal shall ensure that the parties are given a reasonable opportunity to present their observations on any submission by the third person.

Article 7

Submission by a Non-disputing Party to the Treaty

1. The arbitral tribunal shall, subject to Article 7.4, allow, or, after consultation with the parties, may invite submissions on issues of treaty interpretation from a non-disputing party to the treaty.
2. The arbitral tribunal, after consultation with the parties, may allow submissions on further matters within the scope of the dispute from a non-disputing party to the treaty. In determining whether to allow such submissions, the arbitral tribunal shall take into consideration, among other factors it determines to be relevant, the factors referred to in Article 6.3, and, for greater certainty, the need to avoid submissions which would support the claim of the investor in a manner tantamount to diplomatic protection.
3. The arbitral tribunal shall not draw any inference from the absence of any submission or response to any invitation pursuant to Article 7.1 or 7.2.
4. The arbitral tribunal shall ensure that any submission does not disrupt or unduly burden the arbitral proceedings, or unfairly prejudice any party.
5. The arbitral tribunal shall ensure that the parties are given a reasonable opportunity to present their observations on any submission by a non-disputing party to the treaty.

Annex 3
Schedule of Fees

(All sums stated are in US dollars)

Filing Fee (Non-refundable): US $2,000

A filing fee is applicable to all arbitrations administered by the B&R DRC, and to each claim or counterclaim. Fee includes all taxes.

Administration Fees

The administration fee calculated in accordance with the schedule below applies to all arbitrations administered by the B&R DRC and is the maximum amount payable to the B&R DRC.

Sum in dispute (US$)	Administration fees (US$)
Up to 50,000	3,800
50,001–100,000	3,800 + 2.200% excess over 50,000
100,001–500,000	4,900 + 1.200% excess over 100,000
500,001–1,000,000	9,700 + 1.000% excess over 500,000
1,000,001–2,000,000	14,700 + 0.650% excess over 1,000,000
2,000,001–5,000,000	21,200 + 0.320% excess over 2,000,000
5,000,001–10,000,000	30,800 + 0.160% excess over 5,000,000
10,000,001–50,000,000	38,800 + 0.095% excess over 10,000,000
50,000,001–80,000,000	76,800 + 0.040% excess over 50,000,000
80,000,001–100,000,000	88,800 + 0.031% excess over 80,000,000
Above 100,000,000	95,000

© Zhejiang University Press 2020

G. Wang et al., *Dispute Resolution Mechanism for the Belt and Road Initiative*,
https://doi.org/10.1007/978-981-15-1975-8

The administration fees do not include the following:

- Fees and expenses of the tribunal;
- Usage cost of facilities and support services for and in connection with any hearing (e.g. hearing rooms and equipment, transcription and interpretation services); and
- The B&R DRC administrative expenses, and the B&R DRC will charge a minimum administration fee of US$3,800, payable for all cases, unless the Secretary-General otherwise determines.

Arbitrator's Fees

For arbitrations conducted pursuant to and administered under these Rules, the fee calculated in accordance with the schedule below is the maximum amount payable to each arbitrator, unless the parties have agreed to an alternative method of determining the tribunal's fees.

Sum in dispute (US$)	Administration fees (US$)
Up to 50,000	6,250
50,001–100,000	6,250 + 13.800% excess over 50,000
100,001–500,000	13,150 + 6.500% excess over 100,000
500,001–1,000,000	39,150 + 4.850% excess over 500,000
1,000,001–2,000,000	63,400 + 2.750% excess over 1,000,000
2,000,001–5,000,000	90,900 + 1.200% excess over 2,000,000
5,000,001–10,000,000	126,900 + 0.700% excess over 5,000,000
10,000,001–50,000,000	161,900 + 0.300% excess over 10,000,000
50,000,001–80,000,000	281,900 + 0.160% excess over 50,000,000
80,000,001–100,000,000	329,900 + 0.075% excess over 80,000,000
Above 100,000,001–500,000,000	344,900 + 0.065% excess over 100,000,000
Above 500,000,000	605,000 + 0.040% excess over 500,000,000, up to a maximum of 2,000,000

Emergency Interim Relief Fees

Under these Rules, an application for emergency interim relief must be accompanied by a payment of the following:

1. Administration fees for emergency arbitrator applications (non-refundable): US$ 5,000 (fees include all taxes).
2. The emergency arbitrator's fees and deposits: The deposits toward the emergency arbitrator's fees and expenses shall be fixed at US$30,000, unless the Secretary-General of the B&R DRC determines otherwise pursuant to the schedule to these Rules. The emergency arbitrator's fees shall be fixed at US $25,000, unless the registrar determines otherwise pursuant to the schedule to these Rules.

Challenge Fee (Non-refundable)

A party submitting a notice of challenge shall make payment of the following challenge fees: US$2,000 (fees include all taxes).

Appendix 1
The Dispute Resolution Mechanism for the Belt and Road Initiative

Guiguo Wang

The implementation of the Belt and Road Initiative involves trade, investment, IP rights, sanitary and phytosanitary standards, product safety standards, tax laws, competition laws, and so on. It requires the cooperation of governments and the participation of enterprises and individuals along the B&R. The cooperation, on the one hand, needs the relevant countries' coordination at political, legal and administrative levels and, on the other hand, needs to regulate the activities of enterprises and individuals. In such an enormous economic cooperation process of the Belt and Road Initiative, disputes are inevitable. Consequently, how to settle the disputes is in fact an issue that the Belt and Road Initiative must face.Broadly speaking, disputes related to the Belt and Road Initiative may be divided into those between governments, between enterprises, and between a government and an enterprise. If it is classified by the nature of the underlying transaction, such disputes may be subdivided into commercial disputes, international trade disputes and investment disputes.

Traditionally, disputes arising from transactions between enterprises (including those between an enterprise and an individual) are treated as commercial disputes, and those arising from intergovernmental cooperation as disputes between contracting parties. The other kind of disputes is called investor-state disputes that are disputes between a foreign investor and its host government. Such kind of disputes is more complicated as an enterprise may have a dispute with the host state regarding tax issues or an administrative action of the state. Unless a relevant dispute involves obligations under a treaty, such disputes can only be settled by the local court in the country where the enterprise is located or in a manner permitted by the local laws. However, where an enterprise–government dispute involves an obligation under the World Trade Organization (WTO) agreements or a free trade agreement and where the enterprise believes that a local government's action or omission violates such an obligation, the dispute may either be of a trade nature, or belong to category of investment disputes. In the case of the former, the enterprise may only seek to have the dispute resolved via the government of its own country, in which no compensation may be paid to the affected enterprise. If the dispute is of an investment nature and there exits an investment agreement or a free trade

© Zhejiang University Press 2020

G. Wang et al., *Dispute Resolution Mechanism for the Belt and Road Initiative*,
https://doi.org/10.1007/978-981-15-1975-8

agreement (with Investment Chapter) between the states where the enterprise is incorporated and the state where that enterprise has the place of business, that is, host state, the enterprise, as a foreign investor, may be entitled to the settlement of dispute through arbitration with the host state. Thus, depending on the nature of the dispute, the mechanism and applicable rules for the settlement of such disputes differ. The mechanism for settling the Belt and Road-related disputes should be specifically regulated according to the category of economic cooperation and transaction, and focused at the nature of potential disputes which may arise in relation to the Belt and Road projects. If the dispute is of an investment nature and there exits an investment agreement or a free trade agreement between the state where the enterprise is incorporated and the state where that enterprise has the place of business, that is host state, the enterprise, as a foreign investor, may be entitled to the settlement of dispute through arbitration with the host state. Thus, depending on the nature of the dispute, the mechanism and applicable rules for the settlement of such disputes differ. The mechanism for settling the Belt and Road-related disputes should be specifically designed to regulate the conduct of dispute resolution according to the category of economic cooperation and transaction and the nature of the disputes therefrom.

This paper will first briefly explain the different dispute settlement methods and then discuss the possible choices of and the decisions that ought to be made for the Belt and Road Initiative.

1. Methods for Resolving General Commercial Disputes

A general commercial dispute is an inter-enterprise dispute related to a commercial transaction. The category of such transactions is wide and may include trade, investment, transfer of technology, intellectual property protection, mergers, acquisitions, and divisions of enterprises, sale and purchase of equipment, assignment of concessions, and so on. The shared characteristic of these disputes is that the subject matters are always regulated by the contract between the parties concerned, which includes a method for dispute resolution and governing laws, and so on. It goes without saying that the parties can always choose a court for resolving their disputes. However, if the parties are from different countries and unwilling to resort to a court of either country to settle their disputes, most likely they will choose arbitration as a means to settle their disputes arising out of their contract.

Commercial arbitration consists of institutional arbitration and *ad hoc* arbitration. In institutional arbitration, the legally registered arbitration institution has a physical office, a secretariat and, usually, its own arbitration rules, and so on. *Ad hoc* arbitration is the practice wherein, after the occurrence of a dispute, the parties concerned organize an *ad hoc* arbitral tribunal according to their contract to settle their disputes.

In practice, not all arbitration institutions have their own arbitration rules. Commercial arbitration has now become a very competitive professional business among different institutions. Every arbitration body tries to provide convenient and effective arbitration rules as well as fair and just awards for the purpose of winning recognition and appreciation of the parties so that they would select it as the arbitration body. However, the fairness and justice of an award is very hard to define and determine, so providing convenient and effective arbitration rules has become a practical method of assessing the competence and standing of an arbitration institution.

Currently, the United Nations Commission on International Trade Law (UNCITRAL) Arbitration Rules are widely accepted. They are not only widely adopted in *ad hoc* arbitrations but also adopted by some arbitration institutions, such as the Hong Kong International Arbitration Centre (HKIAC) and the Permanent Court of Arbitration (PCA), as their own arbitration rules.

Arbitration rules concern arbitration procedure. An arbitral tribunal, when analyzing and adjudicating the rights and obligations of parties under a contract, also needs to refer to substantive law, namely applicable law. In contracts for sale and purchase of goods, many contracting parties select the United Nations Convention on Contracts for the International Sale of Goods (CISG) as the governing law of the contract.

The other developing trend in international commercial arbitration is that there is ever increasing emphasis on mediation in the arbitration process or as a separate preliminary step of arbitration proceedings. In practice, very often mediation is combined with arbitration, which has triggered different views on whether an arbitrator should be permitted to serve as a mediator in the same dispute, either before the arbitration proceedings or in the middle of the arbitration proceedings.

Some consider that successful mediation requires the parties concerned to disclose to the mediator the true facts of the dispute as well as their wishes and basic conditions for arriving at a settlement through mediation, including the upper limit of the amount of compensation and the lowest acceptable amount of compensation, and so on. Where mediation fails, such information may impact the award by the arbitral tribunal that has just conducted the mediation. For example, in mediation, a party may make a concession for compromise, but the concession may leave an impression on the arbitral tribunal that the conceding party committed the breach of the contract in question. If mediation fails, the party concerned may be left in an unfavorable position. In addition to the above-mentioned concern, how to ensure enforcement of the mediation agreement is also a very important issue.

Arbitration is a means for resolving disputes. The effectiveness of the arbitral award depends on enforceability of the award. At present, the most influential mechanism for enforcement of an arbitral award is the Convention on the Recognition and Enforcement of Foreign Arbitral Awards of 1958, also known as the New York Convention, which now has 156 contracting parties. According to the New York Convention, all contracting parties have the obligation to recognize and execute foreign arbitral awards made in the other contracting parties. According to the convention, courts of all contracting parties must not carry out a substantive examination of an arbitral award or set aside an arbitral award. Article 5 of the convention specifies several exceptions to the obligation to recognize and enforce arbitral awards. A court of a contracting party, even if it refuses to enforce an arbitral award on the ground that the award falls within any of the exceptions under Article 5, must not set aside the award. It is worth pointing out that it is not easy to establish the existence of an exception specified in Article 5. Therefore, the 1958 New York Convention has been proved to be a considerably effective mechanism for recognition and enforcement of foreign arbitral awards.

2. **Characteristics of and Methods for Settlement of Disputes among the WTO Members**

The WTO has its own dispute settlement mechanism for the settlement of disputes involving trade agreements among member states. The WTO's dispute settlement principle is "putting a person right" and it takes a forward-looking approach. On a member's violation of treaty provisions, the WTO will first require the member to rectify the measures which are not in conformity with treaty obligations, for example, by revising the laws, policies or other administrative measures. As long as a member remedies the situation by eliminating the violation of treaty obligations, it is free from any legal responsibility for the alleged breach. If a member who has violated a treaty obligation refuses to revise the measures as required by the WTO agreements, the prevailing party, namely the affected party, may be authorized to take retaliatory measures.

Retaliatory measures work this way. The affected party may withhold from the country in violation of the WTO obligations, benefits arising out of the WTO agreements such as the most favored nation treatment, national treatment for goods and services, the reduction and waiver of tariffs, and so on. The retaliatory measures are subject to the principle that such action must at first be directed at the same sector of trade or services. If the violation is in the agricultural produce sector, the retaliatory measures should first be directed at agricultural products of the errant member. It is only when the affected member is unable to take retaliatory measures, or it is not practicable to take retaliatory measures, in the agricultural produce sector, that it can suspend benefits of the defaulting party in respect of other products and services. This is called cross-retaliation.

With IPR gradually becoming an important part of trade, abandoning the protection of IPRs of the defaulting member has become an important means of retaliation. Of course, the level of suspension of benefits as a retaliation must be proportionate to the loss caused by the impugned measures, and retaliation should be terminated once the member corrects its measures to comply with the WTO agreements.

Only the member of the WTO has standing in the WTO dispute settlement mechanism. Enterprises and individuals of a member state may bring a complaint against another member state only through their own government. In a case of complaint, the WTO's dispute settlement body will first require the disputing member states to resolve the dispute through discussions and consultation, and submit the dispute to a panel if consultation fails. The consultation should be held within 30 days after the date of filing of the request for consultation. The requested members should acknowledge the receipt of the request for consultation. If a requested member fails to reply within 10 days after receiving the request for consultation, or both parties fail to carry out consultation within 30 days from the date of the request for consultation, the member requesting consultation can directly request the establishment of a panel. This process is aimed at raising the efficiency of the dispute settlement mechanism, and is mandatory.

The panel's report, if not appealed, or the appellate body's report on appeal, is submitted to the dispute settlement body for adoption. The WTO's dispute settlement body adopts the report following the principle of reversed consensus, so all reports submitted will be adopted automatically unless it is rejected unanimously.

Arbitration is also a WTO procedure for dispute settlement, mainly for ruling on the reasonable period for defaulting members to correct the impugned measures, suspension of benefits and whether the level of suspension is equivalent to the level of nullification or impairment suffered by the affected member. In normal situations, the original panel dealing with the case is invited as the arbitrator. The purpose of this provision is to improve efficiency of arbitration, as the panel which dealt with the dispute is familiar with the circumstances of the case.

3. **Characteristics of and Methods for Settlement of Investment Disputes**

An investment dispute is the dispute between a foreign investor and its host country, according to the dispute settlement procedures stipulated in the relevant investment treaty. Previously, developing countries preferred to settle investor-state disputes in courts in the country where the investment made, that is host country. With the development of economic globalization, all countries compete for foreign investments, so the use of host country's court system as the forum for dispute settlement has been gradually abandoned, and third party arbitration has won support for the settlement of investor-state disputes. Such treaty provisions had been accepted by some countries before the mid-twentieth century, but it was not until the 1990s that these provisions attracted widespread attention. One of the reasons for that was Argentina's economic crisis causing governments to adopt emergency measures, affecting the interests of investors that ultimately made Argentina the respondent of several dozen of investment arbitration cases. Successful bringing of arbitration cases between the foreign investors and Argentina greatly encouraged many others to put their disputes with the host countries to international arbitration. It is the current practice that bilateral investment agreements and the investment chapters of the free trade agreements authorize investors to submit their disputes with the host countries to international arbitration, and it has become the norm that investors and host countries settle their disputes through arbitration.

Different from the trade in goods and services, investment arbitration has no uniform multilateral arrangement. All investors start arbitration through bilateral investment agreements or different multilateral arrangements, such as the Energy Charter Treaty and the North American Free Trade Agreement, and so on.

Meanwhile, arbitration institutions having jurisdiction, applicable arbitration rules and applicable laws, and so on, are all stipulated in relevant investment treaties. In practice, except for the provisions of the treaty itself, customary international law has become the applicable law for resolving investor-state disputes.

With regard to selecting the arbitration institution, most bilateral investment agreements and the investment chapter of free trade agreements offer several choices for investors, including consultation and arbitration: Arbitration being either *ad hoc* arbitration (mostly applicable to the UNCITRAL arbitration rules) or institutional arbitration. Institutional arbitration mainly relies on the International Centre for Settlement of Investment Disputes (ICSID) established according to the Washington Convention of 1965. In practice, cases accepted by ICSID are far more than those by other arbitration institutions.

One characteristic of ICSID is that if one of the parties concerned is not satisfied with the arbitration tribunal's award, it can apply for annulment of the award according to the provisions of the Washington Convention. Deviating from the original intent of the Contracting Parties, the ICSID's annulment procedure has become more like an appeal procedure. Perhaps because of this deviation from original intention of the Washington Convention, the annulment procedure has been widely used by both parties to a dispute.

Another characteristic of ICSID is that the Washington Convention stipulates that the Contracting Parties have an obligation to recognize and enforce the arbitration tribunal's awards. Compared with enforcement of awards of other arbitration institutions or *ad hoc* arbitration tribunals that must rely on the New York Convention, arbitration by ICSID has certain advantages, which is one of the reasons why ICSID has been chosen by most investment treaties for resolving investor-state disputes.

4. **Deficiencies of Existing Dispute Settlement Mechanisms**

An accurate and comprehensive evaluation of all dispute settlement mechanisms is a near impossible task. To do so in a short article is even more so. Broadly, international commercial arbitration, the WTO's dispute settlement mechanism and investor-state dispute settlement mechanism, all share the well-rehearsed problems of time-consuming process and high costs. Without doubt, such problems may differ from institution-to-institution and from mechanism-to-mechanism.

With regards to the WTO and investor-state dispute settlement mechanisms, it is generally considered that enforcement of awards is the biggest problem. The WTO has a relatively comprehensive dispute settlement mechanism, but retaliatory measures (to ensure enforcement) must be authorized. In addition, effective retaliation requires support of an economic powerhouse, which is only available to economically strong members. For example, in the US Gambling case, the complainant was authorized to retaliate but had to abandon retaliatory measures in view of the fact that the US could punish it in other international organizations or economic cooperation forums. There are other cases where strong economic powers have refused to comply with their treaty obligations under the WTO system.

Enforcement in investment arbitration is even more difficult. The Washington Convention, in fact, practices a complete self-discipline system for enforcing awards. In other words, it is entirely up to the host country to enforce or not enforce an award, subject, of course, to pressure from the international community.

Needless to say, the biggest problem in investment arbitration is the operation of the arbitration tribunal, which has been criticized mainly for a lack of coordination and the resultant multiplicity of awards on the same subject matter. Different results from different awards of different cases are not problematic. Yet, where relevant international agreement provisions at issue are almost identical and facts are similar, different arbitration tribunals have arrived at inconsistent decisions. Therefore, some consider that an appeal mechanism should be established in investment arbitration for correcting such problems so that a consistent line of decision may follow.

Arbitration tribunals acting as they see fit is another problem in investment dispute settlements. It is impossible for any treaty to make specific provisions on every matter, which gives arbitration tribunals much discretion. The proper exercise of discretion is certainly a function of the arbitration tribunals. Arbitrary interpretation of treaty texts without giving proper consideration to the intent of the contracting parties has become an intractable problem in investment arbitration. The expanded application of the MFN clause is one such example.

An investor-state arbitration tribunal deals with actions and omissions of the host government, and may be said to be virtually exercising a de facto power of judicial review. Yet their conduct of arbitration proceedings remains the same with traditional commercial arbitration, which includes the confidentiality of arbitration. This issue has also come to the attention of the international community at large.

5. **Alternatives for Settlement of the Belt and Road-Related Disputes**

Implementation of the Belt and Road Initiative needs a dispute settlement mechanism which is effective and recognized by the international community. The first issue to be dealt with is the choice of a dispute settlement mechanism. Settling disputes through the courts of the countries along the Belt and Road is not the ideal choice, so alternatives must be explored. As per the above discussion, international arbitration mechanisms can be classified into three basic categories: commercial arbitration, the WTO dispute settlement system and investment arbitration. These mechanisms have their own advantages and disadvantages. Continuing to use such systems means less risk, but will play a lesser role in promoting the Belt and Road Initiative. Meanwhile, some of the mechanisms are impossible to apply. For example, in implementation of the Belt and Road Initiative, country-to-country trade and investment disputes cannot be settled directly through the WTO mechanism.

Based on the above discussion, the establishment of a new dispute settlement mechanism by countries along the Belt and Road is proposed. In addition to the government-to-government disputes, enterprises and individuals should also be able to have their disputes with the government of those countries resolved through the mechanism. The arrangement should address the defects of the WTO dispute settlement mechanism, one of which is not to allow frontline enterprises and individuals in trade to participate in dispute settlements. In addition, many current services and investments are overlapping considerably.

If a dispute settlement system is only responsible for trade disputes but not investment disputes, the disputing parties may have to seek different mechanisms for resolving such disputes, which will not only cause multiple lawsuits but also make it difficult to ensure coordination among such mechanisms invariably resulting in inconsistent approaches and decisions. Under a unified system, trade and investment disputes will be settled following a unified set of rules.

The establishment of a dispute settlement mechanism by the countries along the Belt and Road can also contribute to the consistent interpretation of treaties so as to truly reflect the intent of the contracting parties. Considering the fact that most countries along the Belt and Road are developing countries, the establishment of such an independent dispute settlement mechanism can also help the developing countries to be further integrated into the economic mainstream of the world.

The independent dispute settlement mechanism should have an appeal system. The problems relating to the lack of an appeal mechanism in investment arbitration has been discussed above. In its model investment agreement and position paper on TTIP negotiations, the EU proposed to set up an appellate institution. The China–Australia Free Trade Agreement also specifies that the establishment of an appeal mechanism should be considered in due course. It may be said that the international community now tends to favor the establishment of an appeal system, at least, for investment disputes. As the Belt and Road Initiative covers many countries, its dispute settlement mechanism should be highly forward-looking. The establishment of an appeal procedure is not only of practical significance to the Belt and Road initiative but can also set in motion a global trend.

The establishment of a Belt and Road dispute settlement mechanism may follow the principle of bottom-up or from unofficial to official. In the process, experts from all countries along the Belt and Road should be involved in discussing and proposing the framework, operational procedures, principles and operational rules of dispute settlement mechanism. Once a proposal is formulated, it can be submitted to the governments of the Belt and Road countries for consideration. After the governments of these countries have considered the proposal, government representatives should gather together to negotiate on specific provisions and reach agreement.

6. **Principles and Rules of the Belt and Road Dispute Settlement Mechanism**

As a matter of principle, the Belt and Road dispute settlement mechanism should consider adopting a combination of conciliation and arbitration. The international community views conciliation as an Eastern value and tradition. In practice, all Eastern judicial and arbitration bodies including the Chinese courts and arbitration tribunals attach great importance to conciliation. In some jurisdictions, conciliation is a prerequisite to judicial procedures. For example, all civil lawsuits in Hong Kong must be conciliated first, and only when it is confirmed that the disputing parties have conducted conciliation and the conciliation has failed can a civil case be accepted by a Hong Kong court.

Conciliation is a product of Eastern culture, but it is Western scholars who have done serious theoretical studies of it. Meanwhile, some institutions in Western countries hold various diploma courses on conciliation which has made conciliation much widely known. The Belt and Road Initiative was launched by China. Therefore, emphasis on conciliation in the Belt and Road dispute settlement mechanism should be able not only to carry forward the traditional Chinese culture but also conform to dispute settlement tendencies.

While laying stress on conciliation, we should follow the pick and choose process. First, in order to secure recognition by and support of the international community, the conciliation rules for the Belt and Road should become widely known and win public trust. In this aspect only the UNCITRAL Conciliation Rules and UNCITRAL Model Law on International Commercial Conciliation enjoy such a position.

Moreover, China actively participated in the formulation of the UNCITRAL Conciliation Rules, so it will "gain everything and lose nothing", if the Belt and Road conciliation mechanism adopts the UNCITRAL Conciliation Rules as its own rules.

At the operational level, in line with our proposal that the Belt and Road must adopt a combination of arbitration and conciliation, arbitration and conciliation rules should clearly distinguish between conciliation and arbitration. A conciliator must not serve as an arbitrator subsequent to the failure of conciliation. On the other hand, an arbitrator must not participate in conciliation, if conciliation is initiated in the middle of arbitration proceedings. In this way the Belt and Road's conciliation mechanism will be able to avoid the present difficulties facing conciliation, giving the conciliation system a great step forward. It will surely win the support of the international community.

In order to give full operational effect to conciliation, conciliation rules may stipulate that conciliators as well as parties to conciliation are bound by a strict confidentiality obligation. The evidence submitted by the disputing parties, the positions of any party and concessions made by the parties made in the conciliation stage must not be used as evidence in the arbitration stage.

There is no doubting that conciliation should be promoted as the preferred dispute settlement procedure. However, if conciliation fails, arbitration is the inevitable choice. The first issue would be what kind of arbitration rules should be applied. Currently, the arbitration rules widely recognized by disputing parties which also enjoy the highest public trust are the UNCITRAL Arbitration Rules. The Rules are not only widely applied in *ad hoc* arbitration but also adopted by arbitration institutions such as the Permanent Court of Arbitration and the Hong Kong International Arbitration Centre as their own arbitration rules.

In order to win the widest support of the countries along the Belt and Road, adoption of the UNCITRAL Arbitration Rules is most probably the only choice. Of course, while adopting the rules as a whole, proper revisions must be made according to the actual ground situation.

To meet the international community's criticisms of investment arbitration, the Belt and Road arbitration procedures should emphasize on the principle of transparency. The UNCITRAL Rules on Transparency in Treaty-Based Investor-State Arbitration effective as of April 1, 2014 and the UN Convention on Transparency in Treaty-Based Investor-State Arbitration concluded on March 17, 2015 illustrate that the increase of transparency has become a necessary trend in investment dispute settlement. In this aspect the Belt and Road arbitration mechanism should set an example by adopting the principle of transparency in its dispute settlement mechanism. Where countries along the Belt and Road are the first to sign and adopt the above-mentioned documents, their contributions to arbitration and international economic transactions and cooperation will be of immeasurable importance.

The appellate procedures of the Belt and Road should be formulated with reference to the WTO appellate body rules, practice and procedures and the practice of annulment procedures of ICSID. The rules should aim at correcting the defects of the system of investment arbitration, particularly arbitrary exercise of discretion by arbitration tribunals, unauthorized expansion of jurisdiction and attaching less importance or insufficient importance to the contracting parties' intent, and so on.

The rules should also authorize the appellate body to make decisions mainly on questions of law. Where in a case evidence which could not have been discovered at the initial tribunal hearing has come into light, the appellate body should have the right to verify the relevant facts and evidence in the light of such new evidence.

As discussed above, ineffective implementation of international treaties in relation to trade and investment is an issue that calls for urgent solution. The Belt and Road Initiative's dispute settlement mechanism should address this issue as a top priority. The alternatives include combination of compensation (such as investment arbitration compensation) with retaliation (such as the WTO retaliation mechanism). This alternative, if adopted, may reduce the risks of ineffective implementation of the Belt and Road agreements.

To sum up, formulating an effective dispute settlement mechanism is helpful for the implementation of the Belt and Road Initiative. Formulation of the mechanism should be based on a full consideration and analysis of how existing systems operate, so as to make a common set of rules for trade and investment. These rules should emphasize on combining conciliation with arbitration, maintaining a high degree of transparency, and respecting the intent of contracting parties, which should serve as the core principles for the dispute settlement mechanism of the Belt and Road Initiative. Meanwhile, there must be a separation of persons in conciliation, arbitration and appeal processes: That is, in a particular case these three stages of conflict resolution should be conducted by different experts. By doing so, we will be able not only to highlight characteristics of the Eastern culture but also eliminate the concerns of the international community relating to the inseparability of conciliation from arbitration.

Appendix 2
Developing a Dispute Resolution Mechanism for the Belt and Road Initiative

Daniel Fung

A. Introduction

It is a truism of dispute resolution mechanisms worldwide that developing countries tend to suffer from lack of resources, trained personnel and other systemic incapacity leading to unsatisfactory decisions resulting at times in injustice whereas developed economies labor under sophisticated but expensive dispute resolution mechanisms giving rise often to inequality of arms such that the well-heeled, well-resourced and lawyered-up disputant tends to obtain the desired result at the expense of the less economically powerful.

In addition, sophisticated dispute resolution mechanisms which are rules- and precedent-based tend to lengthen the process resulting in delays, thus giving rise to the adage that "Justice delayed is justice denied".

Given the above, devising a dispute resolution mechanism not just for one country but for several scores of them is necessarily a challenge.

Devising a dispute resolution mechanism to embrace countries and jurisdictions adopting different legal traditions such as civil law, common law and Islamic law creates challenges of a different order.

Creating a dispute resolution mechanism for countries in jurisdictions that are developing as opposed to developed and suffering consequently from chronic lack of capacity gives rise to yet another level of difficulty and complexity.

The foregoing paradigm encapsulates the environment and context under which a dispute resolution mechanism is embraced in the Belt and Road Initiative launched by the People's Republic of China (PRC) in late 2013.

The diverse and multifarious legal traditions and regulations embraced within the B&R countries may be usefully classified into four families:

(1) Civilian which covers principally the countries in jurisdictions forming part of the Soviet Union and its successor organization the Commonwealth of Independent States (CIS) as well as the satellites of the Soviet Union which include the Russian Federation, Mongolia, Kazakhstan, Uzbekistan,

© Zhejiang University Press 2020

G. Wang et al., *Dispute Resolution Mechanism for the Belt and Road Initiative*,
https://doi.org/10.1007/978-981-15-1975-8

Turkmenistan, Kyrgyzstan and Tajikistan as well as the Transcaucasus region forming part of the Soviet Union, including Azerbaijan, Armenia and Georgia and extending into Eastern and Central Europe covering such countries as the Ukraine, Moldova, Belarus, Poland, Romania and Hungary.

To this family would be joined those countries which formed part of the colonial possessions of the former Continental European Imperial Powers such as Vietnam, Cambodia, Laos (all parts of the Napoleonic tradition) and Indonesia (part of the Dutch tradition).

In addition, coming within the same family would be countries which have adopted or been influenced by European continental legal systems such as Thailand and the PRC itself.

(2) Common law countries being principally components of the former British Empire many of which have since the dissolution of Empire joined the successor organization being the British Commonwealth such as Singapore, Malaysia, Myanmar, Bangladesh, India, Nepal, Bhutan, Sri Lanka, Pakistan and Kenya.

To this family would be joined other countries which have undergone colonial or protectorate experience under American tutelage such as the Philippines.

(3) Islamic law countries including Afghanistan, Iran, Saudi Arabia and the Maldives.
(4) Mixed or hybrid jurisdictions incorporating elements of civilian, common law and Islamic law such as Brunei, Bahrain, Qatar, Oman, Yemen, Jordan, Egypt and the United Arab Emirates.

First, one striking feature of B&R countries is that they comprise overwhelmingly developing economies. The challenges of devising a fair, just, affordable, cost-efficient and expeditious dispute resolution mechanism for the B&R are particularly acute.

Given that most B&R countries are developing economies which enjoy neither sophisticated legal systems nor strong, developed, mature legal traditions, setting up a sophisticated and complex dispute resolution system for the B&R is not the obvious solution.

Secondly, given that the majority of B&R countries do not hail from a common law tradition, imposing an Anglo-American common law arbitration system cannot be an appropriate solution either.

Thirdly, given that the vast majority of B&R countries and the parties involved in a dispute (apart from Chinese SOEs and MNCs) would not necessarily be financially well-resourced, lengthy and sophisticated dispute resolution proceedings may not be the right answer.

Fourthly, lengthy dispute resolution proceedings may delay or derail investment projects which would defeat the primary purpose of the B&R.

Bearing the above in mind, the silver lining to this formidably black cloud is the stark fact that, faced with this paradigm, we are nevertheless faced with no choice but to devise a fair, just, speedy, affordable and cost-efficient dispute resolution mechanism to cover three areas:

(1) Commercial disputes between corporations and enterprises;
(2) Investment disputes between investors and states;
(3) Inter-state disputes.

The challenges inherent in devising an appropriate dispute resolution mechanism vary in relation to each of the above categories.

B. Commercial Arbitration

In addressing commercial arbitration between corporations and enterprises, we have already noted the inherent disadvantages and deficiencies of the Anglo-American system which entails massive discovery and production of documents, an adversarial process which by its very nature is time-consuming, particularly when it comes to cross-examination of witnesses (including experts) leading to considerable expense as well as entailing a substantial risk of delay.

There is clearly room for an Anglo-American style or type of dispute resolution in developed countries and jurisdictions which puts a premium on quality of analysis leading to a fair and just outcome. However, even in developed economies and jurisdictions, there has already arisen over the past decade a backlash and resistance to over-lawyered and overly sophisticated, complex and technical proceedings.

One must not forget that a generation ago arbitration was conceived of as a speedy, economical and non-technical (in the sense of a simple, direct approach which is not over-lawyered) alternative to litigation, and then regarded as an expensive and highly technical process overly burdened by rules of evidence and case precedents.

The irony of the past 30 years is that arbitration has fallen victim to its own success in that the industry, originally conceived of being a simple and inexpensive process, has become so lucrative that it has been hijacked not just by lawyers but predominantly by those from the Anglo-American common law tradition specializing in dispute resolution such that arbitration is now often more expensive than litigation in specialized commercial courts in London or Hong Kong with no obvious advantage in terms of speed of resolution either.

The current mechanism relies on arbitrators to exercise control over the proceedings. In practice, however, even relatively simple cases tend to transmogrify into fully-blown processes. This is because:

(1) Parties tend, by dint of human (or lawyerly) nature, to seek increasing opportunities to develop or present their respective cases and arguments;

(2) Arbitrators tend to eschew a strict implementation of the agreed timeline for fear of a challenge by the losing party complaining that its right to present its case has been unfairly curtailed.

To address this problem, we propose that arbitration institutions establish a set of default procedures from which deviation would only be permitted upon agreement by the parties or by order of the arbitrators.

1. **Proposed Default Procedures**

- One round of pleadings only, unless the respondent raises a counterclaim, in which case the claimant should be entitled to file a reply;
- Production of documents should be limited to documents mentioned in the pleadings or witness statements;
- A deadline should be set for interlocutory applications;
- No oral evidence unless leave is granted by tribunal;
- Hearing should normally be set down for 1–3 days only;
- Single expert to be appointed by tribunal;
- Arbitration should be conducted in one single language with translation to be supplied by the party requiring such translation at its own expense;
- A standard timeframe may be set for submission of pleadings and witness statements and parties may apply for extension of time if needed.

2. **Summary Procedure**

If the claim is modest in size, then a summary procedure may be adopted. Alternatively, parties may also agree to adopt such a summary procedure. The proposed summary procedure is as follows:

- Sole arbitrator;
- Claimant to submit pleadings together with all supporting evidence;
- Respondent to submit its defense together with all supporting evidence;
- Sole arbitrator to decide whether any further rounds of pleadings/evidence are required;
- No oral hearing.

3. **Key Features of the Proposed Model and Justification**

(1) An Inquisitorial Approach

The great advantage of the B&R is that one starts with a tabula rasa thereby forcing a reconsideration whether the Anglo-American common law approach to dispute resolution is the most appropriate for B&R countries given the iron law that over-sophistication tends to increase expense and result in delay.

Given the predominance of non-common law jurisdictions among B&R countries, there is much to commend an inquisitorial approach as opposed to an adversarial one.

The inquisitorial system may be broadly defined as a system which seeks to arrive at the truth of the controversy via investigation and examination of relevant evidence. An adversarial system, on the other hand, seeks to arrive at forensic truth through open competition between the parties each striving to make the most persuasive argument for their case.

In international arbitration, arbitrators are given considerable discretion to conduct proceedings in such a manner as they see fit. The approach adopted tends to turn on the professional background and training of tribunal members as well as that of the parties. It is not uncommon for a hybrid approach to be adopted, especially when members of the tribunal hail from different jurisdictions, more especially from disparate legal traditions.

An inquisitorial approach is likely to be comparatively speedy and cost-efficient and would better suit the requirements of B&R countries as well as serve the object of the B&R itself.

(2) Restricted Approach to Discovery and Production of Documents

Under Anglo-American practice, it is not uncommon for parties to zealously make extensive requests for discovery and production of documents, much of which may be neither necessary nor expedient.

In commercial cases, it is common for both parties to be in possession of the key documents of the transaction. Experience shows that a restricted approach to discovery and production of document will not normally affect the parties' ability to present their respective cases.

To ensure a just result, the tribunal under the proposed B&R dispute resolution model would nevertheless retain residual power to order a party to produce evidence if strictly necessary.

(3) Short Hearings

Given increasing reliance on electronic communication and the consequent relative ease of production of documentary evidence by way of e-mails or text messages, the role of oral testimony would be of decreasing importance.

Parties wishing to challenge a witness's evidence may do so by challenging the witness statement, thereby obviating the need for extensive or lengthy cross-examination.

The tribunal would retain a residual discretion to allow parties to call witnesses where necessary.

(4) Language

One of the most difficult but important challenges to devising a speedy and cost-efficient B&R dispute resolution process is the issue of language of proceedings. B&R countries embrace over 60% of humanity and a Babel of languages which render acute the issue of choice of language of proceedings and cry out for a simple and cost-efficient solution.

Given that bilingual or multilingual proceedings are lengthy, complex and costly and that translation of documentary evidence can also be extremely expensive, it is proposed that proceedings be conducted in a single language with the disputing parties being given liberty to engage at their expense their own translator if desired. Given the reality of English as the predominant global language not just for trade, commerce and investment but also for research and communication in general, good practical common sense argues in favor of English being adopted as the default language of proceedings unless the parties agree otherwise.

(5) Single Expert

Again in the interest of speed, affordability and cost-efficiency, it is proposed that the principle of a single expert be adopted as the default position.

B&R investment projects are likely to engage infrastructure, construction, agriculture, natural resources and energy. Disputes arising in these areas usually require expert evidence, which can be very costly. If each party were allowed to appoint its own expert, disputes would almost inevitably arise leading to challenges to the independence and impartiality of the experts.

Our proposed solution is to adopt a single expert as the default position.

4. Opting Out of the Setting-aside Procedure

The next question to be addressed is the imperative of adopting a simplified procedure to avoid multiplicity of hearings.

Although an award can only be set aside on limited grounds, the setting-aside proceedings could be time-consuming and is often employed by losing parties as a delaying tactic. As the grounds for setting aside the award is substantially the same as those for non-enforcement, it may not be necessary to undergo two sets of proceedings before an award can be enforced.

Given the problem of delay, some states have amended their arbitration law to allow parties to opt out of the setting-aside procedure, for example, France, Switzerland and Belgium. B&R countries should be encouraged to amend their domestic law to enable parties to opt out of the setting-aside procedure. Further, parties may be encouraged to choose seats of arbitration which allow for such opting out in the interest of arriving at a swift resolution of disputes.

C. **Investment Arbitration and Inter-State Arbitration**

Turning now to investment arbitration and inter-state arbitration, this generates a different set of challenges from commercial disputes.

Time-consuming: On average an ICSID arbitration would last for 3 years and 8 months. In some cases it could take up to 2 or 3 years to resolve a jurisdictional challenge. Taking as an example the recent decision in Ping An Insurance v

Belgium, the notice of arbitration was filed in September 2012 but the award on jurisdiction only came out on April 30, 2015.

High legal costs: It is reported that the average claimant costs in the 55 ICSID arbitrations concluded between 2011 and 2015 was US$5,619,261.74. The combined costs of the claimant and the respondent exceed US$8 million.

Limited access: It is not uncommon for developing countries to limit their exposure to investment arbitration by adopting restrictive arbitration clauses in Bilateral Investment Treaties (BITs). Taking China as an example, its first- and second-generation BITs contain restrictive arbitration clauses which only allow a certain type of disputes (typically expropriation) to be submitted to arbitration.

Piecemeal manner: The dispute resolution mechanism varies according to the BIT in question. There is no uniform mechanism between B&R countries to resolve investment disputes. For example, Singapore–Jordan BIT provides for ICSID arbitration while Singapore–China BIT provides for *ad hoc* arbitration.

Uncertainty: ICSID tribunals reach different conclusions on the same issues. An often cited example is the sharply divided jurisprudence on the issue of whether a most favored nation (MFN) clause can be applied to procedural matters.

Enforcement problem: Enforcement against state parties is extremely difficult due to state immunity. At present, the majority of ICSID awards are voluntarily complied. While the WTO has a relatively comprehensive dispute resolution mechanism, retaliatory measures must be authorized. In additional, effective retaliatory measures require support of an economic powerhouse, which is only available to economically strong members.

The solution is to establish a uniform mechanism to address investment disputes arising in the B&R context.

1. **Multilateral Investment Treaty or Model BIT**

Instead of submitting investment disputes to the ICSID regime or *ad hoc* arbitration, there needs to be a separate mechanism specifically tailored for investment disputes in the B&R context.

A multilateral investment treaty on B&R-related disputes would be conducive to a more efficient dispute resolution mechanism. Alternatively, a Model BIT (like the UNCITRAL Model Law on International Commercial Arbitration) tailored for B&R countries can be published and member states can adopt the Model BIT with necessary amendments. The Model BIT can deal with both investor-state and inter-state disputes.

If this can be achieved, investment arbitration and inter-state proceedings will be significantly shortened because any issues regarding interpretation of treaty can be dealt with very quickly.

The above tasks can be initiated by, among others, the Asian Infrastructure Investment Bank (AIIB), the Silk Road Fund, International Academy of the Belt and Road or other competent authorities of the Chinese government.

2. **Sanction for Non-compliance of Award**

To address deficiencies in the current enforcement mechanism, it is proposed that a member state which fails to comply with an investment arbitration award may be sanctioned by reducing its credit rating at financial institutions which provide funding for the investments in B&R countries. This would incentivize member states to comply with the award.

Financial institutions such as AIIB or the Silk Road Fund would have an incentive to support the enforcement mechanism as they have an undoubted interest in encouraging due performance of contracts in B&R projects. Further, non-compliance of an arbitral award may be an implication that the member state has a tendency to default.

3. **Adopt the Proposed Default Procedures**

Last but not least, the proposed B&R dispute resolution procedure should also be adopted in investment arbitrations.

D. **Third-Party Funding**

A final consideration is the advent of third-party funding as to which we stand on the cusp of a major global dispute resolution mechanism revolution in the sense that third-party funding is likely to transcend and transform, for good or ill, the nature and texture of dispute resolution both within countries and transnationally.

Third-party funding arose predominantly as a first world or developed economy phenomenon but is likely to impact developing economies in turn. B&R countries are not immune from this process and will likely face increasing challenges arising from this phenomenon in the years to come.

The rationale for permitting third-party funding of dispute resolution is the simple proposition that dispute resolution in the first world or developed economies has become so sophisticated, complex and expensive as to lie beyond the reach of all but publicly listed companies, MNCs, SOEs and governments. The disenfranchised resemble not so much the traditional sandwich class of the late twentieth century but rather, in this age of globalization and rising inequality, everyone saves for the 1% or the 0.1% of a global elite.

Looked at in this perspective, third-party funding fulfills a pressing need for the delivery of justice on the premise that unaffordable justice amounts to justice denied.

Hence the phenomenon of third-party funding which arose first in Australia is now sweeping the United States, United Kingdom and Singapore.

That said, it can be seen that third-party funding is not just a first world or developed economy phenomenon, it is predominantly an Anglo-American or common law phenomenon.

The social economic factors propelling third-party funding are less acute (albeit not unknown) in European continental systems and have yet to reach the developing world. However, as noted above, the developing world is by no means inoculated against the spread of this phenomenon. An easy entry point is investor-state arbitration where the investor is not blessed with pockets as deep as those possessed by the opposing state.

The problems inherent in third-party funding are too complex and carry a sufficient number of unknowns at this stage to allow for an exhaustive analysis of the issue. Indeed, it is a fit subject for a separate paper and a separate conference.

Suffice it to say for present purposes that if a speedy, affordable and cost-effective dispute resolution mechanism could be devised for B&R countries, the pressure for third-party funding may be ameliorated, if not eliminated.

Appendix 3
Policy Paper on National Good Offices

Locknie Hsu

A. Introduction and Summary of Proposal

The purpose of this policy paper is to set forth the idea of a non-adversarial investor grievance mechanism for the Belt and Road economies. As a large number of countries and their businesses are being linked through the B&R Initiative, it is inevitable that, with time, some grievances or disputes will arise. Some of these may be between investors from B&R countries who have a grievance or complaint against a B&R host country.

This proposal is to put forward the establishment of a B&R investor grievance resolution mechanism at the national/regional level for B&R participant countries. Such a mechanism aims to (a) provide a B&R host country with an early notice of a problem faced by a B&R investor and (b) provide such a B&R host country with an opportunity to resolve the dispute amicably and to prevent unnecessary escalation of the problem, if possible. It is therefore the first step for a foreign B&R investor, who can first try to have its unhappiness addressed at the national level. It is non-adversarial as conceived, and is primarily a problem-solving mechanism.

A clear, transparent, accessible and robust system to detect and resolve foreign investment complaints and potential disputes early can contribute to building good governance practices and a strong rule of law approach in B&R countries.

B. Background and Explanation

In many investor complaints against host countries, the complaints have been allowed to develop and escalate into highly adversarial and contentious litigation and arbitration proceedings. Such proceedings can lead to high legal costs, take a great deal of time, delay or derail the commercial transaction or project, or result in an outcome that does not necessarily meet the needs of both sides. In addition, in such situations, the aggrieved investor and the host country often can no longer have a cordial working relationship.

© Zhejiang University Press 2020

G. Wang et al., *Dispute Resolution Mechanism for the Belt and Road Initiative*,
https://doi.org/10.1007/978-981-15-1975-8

In the context of the B&R, a system which facilitates early, speedy, fair and affordable resolution of investor grievances in a non-adversarial manner can contribute to continuity of transactions and projects. This is particularly useful for long-term projects (such as in infrastructure or natural resource development) where continuity of working relationships may be desirable.[1]

This paper therefore proposes the establishment of such a "first step" B&R national/regional mechanism. Such a mechanism is not without precedent. In some countries, the mechanism takes the form of an independent and neutral person called an "Ombudsman". An example of this can be seen in R.O. Korea, which has established by law the Office of the Foreign Investment Ombudsman (OFIO).[2] The R.O. Korean system includes several other features to address investor complaints early, such as the "Home Doctors" system which deploys consultants to foreign-invested companies or regions to receive and resolve investor grievances. The OFIO meets with foreign investors to hear complaints at both the macro (macro-level issues such as deregulation and communication channels with the government) and micro (specific investors' grievances) levels. Quarterly reports on grievance handling cases resolved by the OFIO are also published. According to the OFIO, the number of cases it handled increased by 5.7% (to 462 cases) in 2015, year on year, the highest since its establishment. This multifaceted model offers interesting aspects which merit study by B&R countries. It is noted that in other countries, the term "Ombudsman" is not necessarily a familiar one and may not be in use.

In Myanmar, for example, the new Foreign Investment Law contains an investment grievance mechanism to prevent escalation of an investor's dispute with the state, which does not use such a term.[3]

---

[1]See generally UNCTAD, *Investor-State Disputes: Prevention and Alternatives to Arbitration* (2010) at http://unctad.org/endocsdiaeia200911_en.pdf.

[2]See Foreign Investment Ombudsman Annual Report 2015, at kmgw.kmu.ac.kr:8089/wo00149/1000343/15c20b9e90c64919a5d3408e5794c891 (with grateful acknowledgement to Professor Lori Yi for this link).See also the brief record of discussion about the Korean system here: http://www.singaporelawblog.sgblogarticle/145.

[3]The law was passed in January 2016 (see http://www.burmanet.org/news/2016/01/07/the irrawaddy after much deliberation investment law approved by parliament ksaw hsu mon/); see Section 20: "Investment Grievance Mechanism".

(1) The Union Government shall establish and manage a mechanism to systematically track, respond and try to address enquiries and grievances related to the effective implementation of this law before they escalate into legal disputes.

(2) The purpose of the grievance mechanism is to prevent the occurrence of disputes by offering a mechanism for early detection of issues and grievances and their resolution before they can escalate into a dispute. As such the grievance mechanism is separate from and complements the dispute settlement mechanism as provided for in Section 21 of this act.

Note also that under Myanmar law, investors have a number of duties to observe; see http://www.dica.gov.mm/en/foreign-investment.

Under a system established in Vietnam in early 2014, the Ministry of Justice has been designated as the lead agency to coordinate resolution of disputes arising between foreign investors and the Vietnamese Government on the basis of investment guarantee agreements.[4]

Under this system, government agencies, organizations and individuals work together under the coordination in order to resolve the particular investor complaint. Such coordination includes addressing matters such as the following:

1. Resolution of complaints, consultancy, negotiation, conciliation for disagreements, conflicts with foreign investors.
2. Elaboration and implementation of strategies, plans to resolve international investment disputes.
3. Supply of related information, dossiers, evidences and documents in the service of resolution of international investment disputes.
4. Appointment of persons who have full capacity in agencies, organizations to participate in resolution of international investment at the request of the presiding agency.
5. Implementation of affairs related to resolution of international investment disputes in proceeding stage of international arbitration or competent foreign tribunals.
6. Implementation and coordination in handling of contents related to executing judgments, decisions of international arbitration or competent foreign tribunals.[5]

The first step above is the example that is most pertinent to the present proposal paper. The system provides an early warning system where a dispute with a foreign investor may arise and allows coordinated actions to address complaints with a view to resolution.[6] Prior to the matter escalating to a legal action, the relevant state agencies, organizations and individuals "may conduct negotiation, conciliation with foreign investors according to the plan approved by their directly superior agencies after they have opinion of the legal representative agency of government".[7] Any signs of violations of laws by the investor may also be highlighted. This early-warning and early-resolution/coordination system focusing on the non-litigious stage of a dispute offers an interesting case study for B&R countries to consider.

[4]See Article 5(2),Regulation on Coordination in Resolution of International Investment Disputes, Decision No. 04/2014/QD TTg, 14 January 2014, which establishes this system. See also generally: http://globalarbitrationnews.com/new decision defining the roles of state bodies in the settlement of international investment disputes 20150202/. [Other agencies coordinate other types of disputes involving the Vietnamese Government, such as the Ministry of Finance.]

[5]See Article 4.

[6]See Article 10.

[7]See Article 10.3.

In international dispute resolution systems such as that under the World Trade Organization[8] and those under certain FTAs, this may take the form of good offices, albeit on a voluntary basis.[9] In one definition by UNCTAD the term is explained as follows: "Good offices involves the use of a third party to liaise with the disputing parties and to convey to each party the views of the other on the dispute. The third party plays no part in suggesting solutions to the dispute".[10]

As this term is used in the WTO and other non-WTO agreements, it could be a suitable name for the B&R first-stage mechanism, as it is familiar to many and a relatively neutral name. The B&R good offices mechanism could be made mandatory, and would provide a facility for a neutral party to hear an investor's complaint and to facilitate communications at an early stage, in an effort to resolve any miscommunication, misunderstanding or other unhappiness, if possible, by handling the matter in an amicable and non-litigious setting.

The following are reasons for advocating a system of good offices—using this name tentatively for the present discussion under the B&R Initiative, and set out some core considerations for B&R countries to adopt. (Further features—whether drawn from the examples of models mentioned above or from elsewhere—can then be included if they are deemed useful.)

First, the B&R Initiative offers an opportunity to forge consensus among B&R countries to each designate or establish (if there is none yet) an independent investor grievance mechanism at the national or regional level.

---

[8]See the WTO, *Understanding on Dispute Settlement*, Article 5, which provides as follows:
Article 5 Good offices, Conciliation and Mediation

1. Good offices, conciliation and mediation are procedures that are undertaken voluntarily if the parties to the dispute so agree.
2. Proceedings involving good offices, conciliation and mediation, and in particular positions taken by the parties to the dispute during these proceedings, shall be confidential, and without prejudice to the rights of either party in any further proceedings under these procedures.
3. Good offices, conciliation or mediation may be requested at any time by any party to a dispute. They may begin at any time and be terminated at any time. Once procedures for good offices, conciliation or mediation are terminated, a complaining party may then proceed with a request for the establishment of a panel.
4. When good offices, conciliation or mediation are entered into within 60 days after the date of receipt of a request for consultations, the complaining party must allow a period of 60 days after the date of receipt of the request for consultations before requesting the establishment of a panel. The complaining party may request the establishment of a panel during the 60-day period if the parties to the dispute jointly consider that the good offices, conciliation or mediation process has failed to settle the dispute.
5. If the parties to a dispute agree, procedures for good offices, conciliation or mediation may continue while the panel process proceeds.
6. The Director-General may, acting in an *ex-officio* capacity, offer good offices, conciliation or mediation with the view to assisting Members to settle a dispute.

[9]See, for example, Article 20.6 of the China-Korea FTA.

[10]UNCTAD, *Dispute Settlement: Investor-State* (2003), at page 21.

The advantages of such a mechanism are as follows:

1. There will be a clear point of contact for a B&R investor who wishes to surface its issues to the host B&R country.
2. The B&R host country has an opportunity to use a non-adversarial forum to discuss the issues with the investor. Such discussions may be held confidentially (to promote frank discussions). Such a step can provide an avenue for clarification of the issues and for a neutral fact-finding exercise, particularly if the grievance involves a state agency that has been either unresponsive to or shown low interest in engaging with the aggrieved investor.
3. The mechanism gives the host country a first opportunity to resolve the issues and prevent unnecessary escalation. The mechanism will allow the forging of solutions that could be "win–win" in the sense that the solutions are not limited only to conventional legal remedies (such as a one-shot payment of a large quantum of damages), but could include other permitted and legitimate "in kind" remedies. This mirrors the approach advocated in mediation practice, in seeking tailored solutions that best meet all disputing parties' needs and interests. This also takes into account that B&R countries vary significantly in economic development and may have a variety of options to offer by way of solutions.
4. An effective solution formed this way can promote continuity of the relationship between the investor and the host country, and in the B&R context, can allow a project (e.g. building or infrastructure) to carry on without too much delay or too many legal costs.

A second feature of the proposed mechanism is independence. This is necessary to ensure its credibility and effectiveness. While the mechanism may (at the choice of the B&R countries) involve an official body or an officer of the government, it must, in order to be independent and be seen to be independent, also involve at least one other independent, non-government person of that country. This could, for example, be a non-government person (e.g. head of an international chamber of commerce, a senior academic with a good understanding of international commerce or a former senior civil servant who has commercial or industry expertise). Such a person can provide an outsider's view as well as provide additional ideas on possible commercially oriented solutions. Such an outside person should be engaged on a pro bono basis, and all persons implementing this mechanism (including the independent outside party) should declare any actual or perceived conflicts of interest in relation to any dispute, and recuse themselves should there be any actual conflict of interest in a given case.

A third feature relates to the training of person(s) in the good offices mechanism. The choice of person(s) implementing the mechanism is critical. If the persons do not have strong skills of communication, agency and issue coordination or problem solving, or are not familiar with how to craft solutions using all available options, there will be a higher risk of escalation of the dispute beyond the mechanism (especially where a difference in cultures exist), into possibly more contentious and costly proceedings. In essence, the person(s) will need to have many of the skills that good mediators have, such as the ability to listen and communicate effectively, to build relationships, and to see and craft creative solutions. If B&R countries agree to establish such a system of "good offices" mechanisms, it will be important to ensure that the person(s) involved in the mechanisms be adequately trained in communication (to hear out the grievance well and to communicate options and ideas well and in an amicable fashion), practical problem-solving methods to help for commercial parties, and effective issue and personnel coordination and case management.

A fourth feature proposed addresses the ensuring of best practices of such mechanisms. This feature proposes that regular (perhaps annual in the first two years, and then biennial) meetings of all persons in charge of national/regional B&R good offices mechanism be held for the following purposes:

1. Sharing of experiences and best practices.
2. Peer review of each other's practices and output. Peer review can be a useful and respectful way to share ideas and to help each other improve. It is used in various contexts in ASEAN, the OECD and in the WTO system.

A fifth feature would be to have established timeframes or goals for problem-solving. This is necessary because if the good offices mechanism is too slow, ineffective or unresponsive, there is a high risk that the aggrieved investor may seek alternatives which could escalate the dispute to a more contentious setting. In this regard, there may also be a need to train those implementing the mechanisms to be highly effective in issues and case management. Another purpose for including a relatively short timeframe is to ensure that truly contentious cases which cannot be resolved at this level will be able to proceed speedily to the next step, whether that is mediation, adjudication or arbitration, or any other method.

Finally, clear information on each good offices mechanism, contact point, case handling processes and non-confidential information on successfully resolved cases should be made publicly accessible (e.g. via the Internet) so that B&R investors and potential investors may easily locate such information. Such a system would help promote transparency, early opportunities for disputes to be resolved amicably and help reduce costs for handling complaints. For B&R countries it would also contribute to building good governance and implementation of laws and regulations.

C. **Proposed System**

The proposed system therefore consists of the following:

1. Establishment (by agreement of B&R countries that wish to participate) of a system of national/regional good offices facilities;
2. Ensuring independence of the mechanism and its ability to understand commercial parties' needs and to design business-oriented solutions;

3. Ensuring persons implementing the mechanism are trained and highly skilled in commercial problem-solving, coordination, communication and issue/case management;
4. Establishment of a network of the B&R good offices mechanisms and organization of regular meetings among person in charge to allow sharing of information and determining best practices;
5. Setting of timeframes or goals for problem-solving within such mechanisms, to prevent undue delay and to provide an efficient system that is attractive to use. It would be desirable for B&R countries to agree, at a minimum, to a timeframe to be stipulated within an acceptable band, for example, between 1 and 3 months, after which it may be determined that the dispute or complaint has not been resolved at the good offices stage.

It should be noted that the above proposal is made in anticipation of other B&R dispute settlement mechanisms which will similarly promote the aims of a speedy, fair and affordable dispute resolution. Therefore, the above system should be designed and implemented in a manner that is sensitive to the policies of B&R countries which encourage disputing parties to use mediation and arbitration as possible dispute settlement methods where they are appropriate.

Appendix 4
Policy Paper on Mediation

Nohyoung Park Lori Yi Hyunsuk Oh[11]

A. Introduction

The purpose of this policy paper is to set forth the idea of an amicable settlement of disputes arising in the context of the Belt and Road (B&R) Initiative. As more than 60 states are expected to be involved in the B&R Initiative, it is inevitable that certain cross-border disputes will arise between governments and companies, companies and companies, and even between governments and governments. As those states under the B&R Initiative have their own different legal systems, those disputes would be complex and difficult to find a right rule of law to be applicable, which is more important for arbitration and court proceedings. Thus, almost all disputes arising in the B&R context are expected to be amicably settled through mediation, which should not be based on any particular rule of law.

Access to justice is often said to face three problems: the ever-increasing number of disputes brought before courts, the length of time taken by proceedings and the cost. Alternative dispute resolution (ADR), and mediation in particular, has been presented as one of the key solutions for these problems. Mediation may advance social harmony as it engages parties in a process of rapprochement rather than confrontation, and its consensual approach is certain to endure the relationship between the parties in the future as in the past. Thus, ADR generally, and mediation specifically, has been on the agenda of the states in the various parts of the world for a number of years.

Mediation is more appropriate for cross-border disputes as likely to occur in the context of the B&R Initiative where a lot of states are involved with their own different legal systems. Without the agreed substantial rules of law applying to concrete cases or disputes, they may not be properly settled in accordance with any particular rule of law, which may not be agreed to easily among the parties in

[11]Dr. Hyunsuk Oh, R.O. Korea Commercial Arbitration Board, ohs1905@kcab.or.kr.

© Zhejiang University Press 2020

G. Wang et al., *Dispute Resolution Mechanism for the Belt and Road Initiative*,
https://doi.org/10.1007/978-981-15-1975-8

dispute. Nevertheless, they may be properly and amicably settled through mediation which does not need to be based on any particular rule of law. Thus, mediation is suitable for the settlement of disputes arising in the context of the B&R Initiative.

Mediation is also more appropriate for the parties in dispute who have to live together for any reasons. The B&R Initiative, aiming at interconnecting the states through telecommunications, oil pipelines, and so on, should be based on the permanently friendly and amicable relationship although there might be disputes occurring among them. Amicable settlement through mediation may be more appropriate than formal processes such as litigation or arbitration where decisions of right and wrong often pull the parties apart for a long time and even forever. Thus, mediation is suitable for the settlement of disputes arising in the context of the B&R Initiative.

This proposal is to put forward the establishment of the B&R mediation procedures for any cross-border disputes arising in the B&R Initiative. The disputes are expected to be settled through mediation with less time and money and legal rigidity, but with more friendship and prosperity and legal efficiency. The amicable settlement through mediation will positively contribute to the development pursued under the B&R Initiative, and the proposed procedures of mediation provides for a practical and guided way to pursue mediation.

B. **The Major Principles in the Mediation System**

- Objective of Mediation

The objective of mediation is for the parties to settle their disputes amicably without reference to a tribunal, and in this regard mediation should not be a poorer alternative to judicial proceedings or arbitration.

- Scope of Application

The B&R Mediation Rules apply to the mediation of the disputes related to B&R, which include: (a) mediation of investment-related differences or disputes involving the investor(s) and state; (b) mediation of disputes arising out of or relating to a contractual or other legal relationship; (c) mediation of disputes or differences arising between states.

- Nature of Mediation

Mediation is often regarded voluntary in nature, but it may be compulsory or subject to incentives or sanctions, as provided for in the EU Directive (Directive 2008/52/EC). The European Court of Justice (ECJ) also recognized this point in a judgment issued on March 18, 2010 by holding that national law is not prohibited from providing for mandatory out-of-court mediation procedures as a pre-condition for court proceedings. Thus, it may be desirable to require disputes arising in the context of the B&R Initiative to be amicably settled through mediation before resorting to arbitration.

- Confidentiality

Parties in dispute, being private parties or states, want to keep their disputes and their resulting settlement not open to the public. Parties are less likely to have full and frank discussions if the content of mediation might become public later. Confidentiality is fundamental to any mediation.

- Admissibility of Evidence in Other Proceedings

If the mediation does not result in a settlement, neither party is allowed to use the information exchanged during the process in court proceedings or arbitration. Unless the parties agree otherwise, neither mediators nor those involved in the mediation process should be compelled to give evidence in judicial proceedings or arbitration regarding the information arising out of or in connection with a mediation process.

- Enforceability of the Settlement Agreement Resulting from Mediation

Settlement agreements resulting from mediation should be ensured to be enforceable. Enforceability is already provided, for example, in a number of European jurisdictions, by submission to a public notary, or using a court procedure known as homologation. The agreements may be enshrined within a court judgment like in the UK. Mediation, practiced well in the B&R Initiative, would be expected to impact domestic disputes settlement accordingly.

The parties in dispute may formalize the settlement agreement in an arbitral award through expedited arbitration proceedings to ensure the enforceability of the settlement agreement resulting from mediation. As the New York Convention covers only the awards rendered in *ad hoc* or institutional arbitrations, an arbitration proceeding is necessary for the mediated agreement to be formalized as an arbitral award. In this case, the mediator(s) who conduct(s) the mediation should be the arbitrator(s) in the arbitration proceedings for that purpose unless otherwise the parties agree.

- Effect of Mediation on Limitation and Prescription Period

Parties are less inclined to resort to mediation if they are still subject to judicial time limits. Often, therefore, parties will enter into a "standstill agreement" and agree that time bar arguments will not arise for the time spent in mediation. Thus, for amicable settlement to pursue, parties who choose mediation should not be prejudiced by limitation or prescription periods.

- The Code of Conduct for the Mediator

The mediator should help the parties in an independent and impartial way in settling the dispute through an amicable agreement. Independence and impartiality of the mediator should be essential elements of the desired attitude of the mediator. The Code of Conduct for the Mediator should be attached as an annex of the B&R Mediation Rules to suggest the principles of the conduct of the mediator. The mediator should be guided by the Code of Conduct for the Mediator, principles of fairness, objectivity, independence and impartiality.

- Secretariat

As there would be a lot of disputes and the resulting mediated settlement in the B&R Initiative, mediation as a system should be managed impartially and efficiently. For this purpose there should be a secretariat to oversee the process of mediation for assisting to provide for the logistics, to select mediator(s), and keep records, and so on. This establishment should not be big in size, but be located in a rather impartial place for an efficient activity.

Regarding the costs, the secretariat should maintain the standard list of fee and expenses which may be varied depending on mediators in the Working Rules of the B&R Mediation Center. The secretariat should provide the parties with a written information about proposed mediation fees and expenses before the commencement of the mediation proceedings and upon the termination of the proceedings, the secretariat should fix the costs and give a written notice of costs to the parties in dispute.

In conclusion, mediation should be placed at the center of the settlement of cross-border disputes most likely to arise in the context of the B&R Initiative. The proposed rules of mediation are expected to ultimately contribute to the prosperous development of the B&R Initiative.

C. The Belt and Road Mediation Rules (Draft)

The Belt and Road Mediation Rules

Article 1 Scope of Application

1. These Rules apply to as below when the parties have agreed that these Rules shall apply, whether before or after a difference or dispute arises:

    (a) Mediation of investment-related differences or disputes involving investor(s) and state(s);
    (b) Mediation of disputes arising out of or relating to a contractual or other legal relationships; and
    (c) Mediation of disputes or differences arising between states.

2. The parties may agree to exclude or vary any of these Rules at any time. These Rules apply unless otherwise agreed or derogated from by the parties.
3. When any of these Rules is in conflict with a provision of law from which the parties or a party cannot derogate, that provision prevails.

(1) Paragraph 1

Specifies the scope to apply mediation rules, and disputes related to B&R are divided into (i) investment disputes between the investor(s) and state, (ii) disputes arising or relating to a contractual or other legal relationship, and (iii) disputes between states.

Given the nature of "mediation", mediation rules should apply to investment and commercial disputes with the consent of the parties to the disputes. Such consent includes both "prior consent" obtained before any dispute arises and "*ex post facto* consent" obtained after a dispute arises.

Subparagraph (a) concerns investment disputes arising out of investment agreements, for example BITs and FTAs. [§ IBA Mediation Rules Article 1, Paragraph 1][12] With regard to settling disputes related to investment through mediation, it is first required that BITs or FTAs between B&R countries provide for such a mechanism. This may be difficult, as agreements such as a BIT need to be revised. Therefore, given the original purpose of "mediation", it will be preferred if parties to disputes arbitrarily opt for mediation before resorting to investment arbitration, and so on.

Subparagraph (b) concerns commercial disputes arising out of contracts. [§ UNCITRAL Conciliation Rules Article 1, Paragraph 1]UNCITRAL Conciliation Rules Article 1, Paragraph 1: These Rules apply to conciliation of disputes arising out of or relating to a contractual or other legal relationship where the parties seeking an amicable settlement of their dispute have agreed that the UNCITRAL Conciliation Rules apply. Regarding the settlement of commercial disputes through mediation, dispute settlement provisions that provide for "mediation" may be included in investment contracts between countries or between a financial institution, such as the AIIB, and a country, and in commercial contracts between participating companies, when they are concluded for investment related to B&R.

Subparagraph (c) concerns disputes or differences arising between states participating in the B&R Initiative.

[12]IBA Mediation Rules Article 1, Paragraph 1: These Rules are designed for the mediation of investment-related differences or disputes involving states and state entities, whether or not they arise out of contract between the parties.

(2) Paragraph 2

Consent of the parties is required to apply mediation rules. Therefore, the parties may agree not to apply those rules. In addition, it is provided that the parties may also make changes to the rules. [§ IBA Mediation Rules Article 1, Paragraph 2, § UNCITRAL Conciliation Rules Article 1, Paragraph 2]

(3) Paragraph 3

Provided that when some of the mediation rules are not consistent with *jus cogens*, the application of which the parties may not exclude, the latter may prevail. Such *jus cogens* may include investment agreements (such as BITs), laws of each country related to investment (Foreign Investment Promotion Act) and law related to arbitration and civil procedures of each country. [§ IBA Mediation Rules Article 1, Paragraph 3, § UNCITRAL Conciliation Rules Article 1, Paragraph 3]

Article 2 Commencement of Mediation

1. A party wishing to initiate mediation under these Rules shall send a written request to mediate to the other party or parties and to the Secretariat of the Belt and Road Mediation Center (hereinafter "B&R MC").
2. The mediation shall be deemed to have commenced on the date on which the request is registered in the Secretariat of the B&R MC.
3. The request shall contain: (a) a summary of the differences or disputes sufficient to identify the matter giving rise to the request; (b) an identification of any treaty, contract or other legal instrument to which the differences or disputes relate; (c) the names and contact details of the requesting party and its representative(s); and (d) either a reference to the agreement to mediate or an invitation to the other party or parties to mediate under these rules.
4. The mediation shall be held out at least one time in () month(s) from the date of the appointment of mediator(s).
5. Mediation under these Rules may take place at any time, regardless of whether court, arbitration or other dispute resolution proceedings have been initiated.

(1) Paragraph 1

Provides that mediation is commenced when a party notifies the other party or parties that mediation shall be conducted in accordance with the mediation rules with a summary describing the dispute at issue.

The phrase "to the other party or parties and to the Belt and Road Mediation Center" specifies that the notification regarding the commencement of mediation should be made not only to a single party but also to multiple parties on the other side. This provision covers both cases of "one vs. one" and "one vs. many" disputes. It also provides that such notification should be made to the Belt and Road Mediation Center (B&R MC) as well. [§ IBA Mediation Rules Article 2, Paragraph 2]

Unlike Article 2, Paragraph 1 of the UNCITRAL Conciliation Rules,[13] this provision provides that mediation is considered to be initiated when notification to that effect is made to a "mediation institution". This implies the possibility of establishing a standing institution to operate the mediation system in a more effective manner (UNCITRAL Conciliation Rules are focused on *ad hoc* mediation).

According to Article 2, Paragraph 1 of the IBA Mediation Rules, which states "if the parties agreed to mediation under these rules before the differences or disputes arose", mediation can be conducted only when there is an explicit prior consent to mediate in accordance with the mediation rules. However, in this paragraph, the provision of the IBA Mediation Rules has been excluded so that this paragraph can apply where a party requests mediation and the other party agrees to go through the mediation procedures even when there is no prior consent.

(2) Paragraph 2

Specifies the time when mediation is initiated. Mediation is considered to have been initiated when a party registers its request in the B&R MC. According to Article 2, Paragraph 1, Subparagraph (a) of the IBA Mediation Rules,[14] mediation is considered to have been initiated when the request is delivered to the other party. However, it is more reasonable to consider that the mediation is initiated when the request is registered in the mediation institution rather than when the request is received by the other party since there exists ambiguity regarding when the request has been delivered to the other party (if mediation is considered to have been initiated when the request is delivered to the other party, countries adopting the mailbox rule may express opposition).

The time of commencement of mediation assumes legal significance when deciding whether to include mediation procedures in the cooling-off period before resorting to investment arbitration under BITs. In addition, Paragraph 5 states that mediation procedures are terminated when there is no reply from the other party within 30 days from the day when the request is received. As in Paragraph 5, the

[13]UNCITRAL Conciliation Rules Article 2, Paragraph 1: The party initiating mediation sends to the other party a written invitation to mediate under these Rules, briefly identifying the subject of the dispute.

[14]IBA Mediation Rules Article 2, Paragraph 1, Subparagraph (a): 1. The mediation shall be deemed to have commenced: (a) on the date on which the request described in Article 2(2) is received by a party, if the parties agreed to mediation under these rules before the differences or disputes arose.

time of commencement of mediation can be used to calculate the time limit to reply to the request. [§ TTIP Annex III Article 2, Paragraph 1][15]

However, under the B&R Mediation Rules, it is not required that parties submit a "written reply". This is because it is more important to proceed with the procedures, such as selecting mediators, than to submit a *pro forma* written reply in mediation with prior consent of the parties.

(3) Paragraph 3

Specifies what should be included in the request for mediation in accordance with Article 2, Paragraph 3 of the IBA Mediation Rules. Others such as UNCITRAL Conciliation Rules and ICSID Conciliation Rules do not provide such details.

In order for a request for mediation to be made more effectively, such formal matters, which are similar to those included in a request for arbitration, should be specified just as in this provision. A model request for mediation should be attached to the mediation rules in the form of an annex to activate B&R mediation.

(4) Paragraph 4

Provides that mediation should be held at least one time within a certain timeframe.

(5) Paragraph 5

Provides that application for mediation procedures can be made at any time, no matter whether the dispute in question has been submitted for a court trial or arbitration. Unlike investment arbitration, where an applicant has no recourse to arbitration procedures unless any ongoing legal proceedings (domestic remedies) are completed, there is no such limitation in mediation and application can be made at any time.

Except for the IBA Mediation Rules, which provides for the same in Article 2, Paragraph 4, other mediation rules do not have any related provisions.

Article 3 Appointment of Mediator(s)

1. There shall be one mediator unless the parties agree that there shall be three mediators. Where there is more than one mediator, they ought, as a general rule, to act jointly.
2. The parties may designate as a mediator any person whom they consider to be suited to assist them in resolving their differences or disputes as below:

[15] TTIP Annex III Article 2, Paragraph 1: The Party to which such request is made shall provide, within 20 days of receipt of the request, a written response containing its comments on the information contained in the request.

(a) In mediation proceedings with one mediator, the parties shall endeavor to reach agreement on the name of a sole mediator;
(b) In mediation proceedings with three mediators, each party appoints one mediator. The parties shall endeavor to reach agreement on the name of the third mediator.

3. The parties shall jointly designate the mediator within 21 days from the date of commencement of the mediation. The party or parties concerned shall notify to the Secretariat of the B&R MC of the appointment of each mediator.
4. If the parties have not jointly designated a mediator within 21 days, then the Secretary-General of the B&R MC shall appoint the mediator(s) within 14 days.

(1) Paragraph 1

Provides that, unless the parties agree otherwise, there should be only one mediator. Unlike arbitration, a single mediator is appropriate for mediation given its characteristics and the additional costs that may arise if more than one mediator is appointed (e.g. fees of the mediators borne by the parties). However, the parties may agree to appoint three mediators. The ICSID Mediation Rules provide for the appointment of one or three mediators only. As mediation does not require a majority decision by mediators (unlike arbitration), there is no need to limit the appointment cases to only one or three mediators.

(2) Paragraph 2

Specifies how to appoint mediators. The parties are required to agree on a single mediator, or appoint one mediator each and agree on the third mediator for the three-mediator system.

(3) Paragraph 3

Provides that mediators should be appointed within 21 days from the date when mediation is initiated. By setting a clear time limit for appointing mediators, any negligence in the procedures by the other party can be prevented, allowing the procedures to be carried out without undue delay.

However, there exist differences among mediation rules regarding the period. This paragraph refers to the IBA Mediation Rules Article 4, Paragraph 5. The ICSID Conciliation Rules Article 4, Paragraph 1 sets a period of 90 days by providing that "If the commission is not constituted within 90 days after the dispatch by the Secretary-General of the notice of registration", while the UNCITRAL

Conciliation Rules do not contain any time limit regarding the appointment of mediators.

Each party is required to notify the B&R MC of its appointment of mediators under Paragraph 2. [§ ICSID Conciliation Rules Article 5, Paragraph 1][16] Thereafter, the mediation institution will inform the parties and mediators about the mediation procedures and send necessary documents to them. Although the ICSID Conciliation Rules also require the parties to inform the Secretary-General about the "method" of such an appointment, this seems to be difficult to include in the B&R Mediation Rules.

(4) Paragraph 4

If the parties have failed to appoint a mediator within 21 days, the Secretary-General of the B&R MC is required to make such an appointment to ensure the swift and effective conduct of procedures.

The ICSID Conciliation Rules Article 4, Paragraph 1[17] allows the parties to request the Chairman of the Administrative Council of the ICSID, that is, President of the World Bank, to appoint the conciliator or conciliators when the 90-day period has passed.

The IBA Mediation Rules Article 4, Paragraph 7 provides that the Secretary-General of the Permanent Court of Arbitration at The Hague should appoint an institution or person to assist the appointment of mediators, and the TTIP Annex Article 4, Paragraph 3 provides that "The chair of the [institutional body to be defined], or the chair's delegate, shall select the mediator within 5 working days of the request made by either party under Paragraph 2 of this article."

However, it can be considered to provide that the mediation institution should recommend an individual to serve as a mediator rather than appointing one when the parties have failed to appoint a mediator within a certain period. Such provision will show that the B&R Mediation Rules put priority on the autonomy and agreement of the parties. [§ UNCITRAL Conciliation Rules Article 4, Paragraph 2, Subparagraph (a)][18]

[16]ICSID Conciliation Rules Article 5, Paragraph 1: The party or parties concerned shall notify the Secretary-General of the appointment of each conciliator and indicate the method of his/her appointment.

[17]ICSID Conciliation Rules Article 4, Paragraph 1: If the Commission is not constituted within 90 days after the dispatch by the Secretary-General of the notice of registration, or such other period as the parties may agree, either party may, through the Secretary-General, address to the Chairman of the Administrative Council a request in writing to appoint the conciliator or conciliators not yet appointed and to designate a conciliator to be the President of the Commission.

[18]UNCITRAL Conciliation Rules Article 4, Paragraph 2, Subparagraph (a): (2) Parties may enlist the assistance of an appropriate institution or person in connection with the appointment of conciliators. In particular, (a) A party may request such an institution or person to recommend the names of suitable individuals to act as conciliator; or.

Article 4 Independence and Impartiality of Mediator(s)

1. The mediator shall be impartial and independent.
2. A mediator shall not be a national, as being registered in the roster of mediators, of either party, unless the parties agree otherwise.
3. Prior to accepting an appointment as a mediator, any person under consideration shall provide a signed and dated Statement of Independence and Availability to the Secretary-General of the B&R MC.
4. In the Statement of Independence and Availability, the person under consideration shall: (a) disclose any facts or circumstances that might call into question the mediator's independence or impartiality in the eyes of the parties; (b) state the mediator's availability and willingness to conduct the mediation expeditiously and efficiently within the time limit agreed by the parties or, in the absence of such an agreement, within a reasonable time limit following the mediator's appointment.
5. If, during the course of the mediation, a mediator becomes aware of any facts or circumstances that might call into question the mediator's independence or impartiality in the eyes of the parties, the mediator shall disclose those facts or circumstances to the parties in writing without delay.

(1) Paragraph 1

This provision explicitly requires the mediator to be impartial and independent. Neutrality, among all virtues, is the most important for a mediator, and this provision adds more emphasis to it by clearly stating it. [§ IBA Mediation Rules Article 3, Paragraph 1][19]

The UNCITRAL Conciliation Rules Article 7, Paragraph 1 states, "The conciliator assists the parties in an independent and impartial manner in their attempt to reach an amicable settlement of their dispute." And the TTIP Annex Article 4, Paragraph 6 also states, "The mediator shall assist, in an impartial and transparent manner, the parties in bringing clarity to the measure and its possible trade effects, and in reaching a mutually agreed solution." Both emphasizing the mediator's neutrality and impartiality.

(2) Paragraph 2

It is clearly stated that the mediator should be of different nationality from the parties to the dispute. It is reasonable to put such a limitation regarding nationality to guarantee the neutrality and impartiality of the mediator. This could be covered

[19]IBA Mediation Rules Article 3, Paragraph 1: The mediator shall be impartial and independent.

by Paragraph 1, but it is separately specified in Paragraph 2 to emphasize its importance.

The nationality may be determined as being registered in the roster of mediators kept by the Secretariat of the B&R MC.

The ICSID Conciliation Rules and IBA Mediation Rules do not have such a provision. Related provisions are included in the TTIP Annex Article 4, Paragraph 5 and UNCITRAL Conciliation Rules Article 2, Paragraph 2[20].

(3) Paragraphs 3 and 4

Provide that if a person is appointed as a mediator, he/she should sign and submit a statement regarding his/her independence and impartiality. Some mediation rules require that such a statement be submitted to the other party, which seems to envisage *ad hoc* mediation. [§ IBA Mediation Rules Article 3, Paragraph 2][21]

ICSID Conciliation Rules Article 6, Paragraph 2 specifies the details of a declaration.

> Before or at the first session of the commission, each conciliator shall sign a declaration in the following form: "To the best of my knowledge there is no reason why I should not serve on the conciliation commission constituted by the International Center for Settlement of Investment Disputes with respect to a dispute between__________and__________. I shall keep confidential all information coming to my knowledge as a result of my participation in this proceeding, as well as the contents of any report drawn up by the commission. I shall not accept any instruction or compensation with regard to the proceeding from any source except as provided for in the convention on the settlement of investment disputes between states and nationals of other states and in the regulations and rules made pursuant thereto. A statement of my past and present professional, business and other relationships (if any) with the parties is attached hereto." Any conciliator failing to sign such a declaration by the end of the first session of the commission shall be deemed to have resigned.

[20] UNCITRAL Conciliation Rules Article 4, Paragraph 2: In recommending or appointing individuals to act as conciliator, the institution or person shall have regard to such considerations as are likely to secure the appointment of an independent and impartial conciliator and, with respect to a sole or third conciliator, shall take into account the advisability of appointing a conciliator of a nationality other than the nationalities of the parties.

[21] IBA Mediation Rules Article 3, Paragraph 2: Prior to accepting an appointment as a mediator, any person under consideration shall provide a signed and dated Statement of Independence and Availability, in the form annexed as Appendix A, to the parties or any Designating Authority (as defined in Article 4).

There exists a similar system for arbitration as well. This requires a standardized form, and Paragraph 4 specifies the details that need to be included in such a form. It provides that any reasons to doubt the mediator's neutrality, and so on should be written in the statement in advance. [§ IBA Mediation Rules Article 3, Paragraph 3]

(4) Paragraph 5

It is provided that if a mediator learns of any facts or circumstances that might affect his/her independence and neutrality while mediation is being carried out, he/she should not delay in informing the parties of such facts or circumstances in a written form.

This paragraph emphasizes the critical importance of impartiality and neutrality in mediation. [§ IBA Mediation Rules Article 3, Paragraph 4]

Article 5 Resignation and Replacement of Mediator(s)

1. If, during the course of the mediation, a party objects for any reason to a mediator continuing to act, then that party shall notify the mediator, the other party and the Secretariat of the B&R MC. The notification should preferably state the reasons for the objection.
   (a) Any other party to the mediation may comment in writing on the objection within 7 days after the receipt of the objection.
   (b) Following consideration of the objection and any comment on the objection, the Secretariat shall consult directly with the objecting party at a meeting or otherwise to discuss the objection within 7 days of receipt of any comment on the objection, and suggest an appropriate resolution, including the resignation of such a mediator within another 7 days.
2. If a mediator resigns, is incapacitated or otherwise becomes unable to perform the mediator's functions, a new mediator shall be designated pursuant to these rules.

(1) Paragraph 1

Provides that if one party does not want the mediator to continue to serve during the mediation procedures, then that party should notify the other party and mediation institution, and so on, of the reasons for such opposition. The other party may submit comments about such opposition no later than 7 days from the day when it receives the above-mentioned notification. [§ IBA Mediation Rules Article 5, Paragraph 2]

Subparagraph (b) provides that the B&R MC consult directly with the objecting party at a meeting or otherwise to discuss the objection within 7 days after the receipt of any comment on the objection. It will duly suggest an appropriate resolution, including the resignation of such a mediator within another 7 days.

The UNCITRAL Conciliation Rules do not have any provision regarding opposition to the mediator, but the ICSID Conciliation Rules Article 9, Paragraph 1 states, "A party proposing the disqualification of a conciliator pursuant to Article 57 of the convention shall promptly, and in any event before the commission first recommends terms of settlement of the dispute to the parties or when the proceeding is closed (whichever occurs earlier), file its proposal with the Secretary-General, stating its reasons therefor."

(2) Paragraph 2

If the mediator position becomes vacant because the mediator has resigned due to the opposition under Paragraph 1 or has left the position by himself, a new mediator should be appointed in accordance with the procedures as provided for in the Mediation Rules. [§ IBA Mediation Rules Article 5, Paragraph 3]

The ICSID Conciliation Rules Article 11, paragraph 1 also states that "Except as provided for in Paragraph 2, a vacancy resulting from the disqualification, death, incapacity or resignation of a conciliator shall be promptly filled by the same method by which his appointment had been made."

Article 6 Role of Mediator(s)

1. The mediator(s) assist(s) the parties in an independent and impartial manner in their attempt to reach an amicable settlement of their dispute.
2. The mediator will be guided by the Code of Conduct for Mediators, principles of objectivity, fairness and justice, giving consideration to, among other things, the rights and obligations of the parties, the usage of the trade concerned and the circumstances surrounding the dispute, including any previous business practices between the parties.
3. The mediator may conduct the proceedings in such a manner as he considers appropriate, taking into account the circumstances of the case, the wishes the parties may express, including any request by a party that the mediator hear oral statements, and the need for a speedy settlement of the dispute.
4. The mediator shall assist the parties to reach an agreement on a settlement of their dispute on a voluntary basis in which the parties make free, informed and self-determined choices as to the process and the outcome. The parties shall cooperate with the mediator and each other in good faith to advance the mediation as expeditiously and efficiently as possible.
5. With the agreement of the parties, the mediator may consult one or more experts.

(1) Paragraphs 1 and 2

Require the mediator to help the parties in an independent and impartial way in settling the dispute through an amicable agreement. Independence and impartiality of the mediator are mentioned in Article 4, Paragraph 1, but this paragraph once again emphasizes the desired attitude of the mediator. [§ UNCITRAL Conciliation Rules Article 7, paragraphs 1 and 2]

The IBA Mediation Rules Article 7, Paragraph 1 requires similar behavior by stating that "The mediator shall be guided by principles of fairness, objectivity, independence and impartiality", which encompasses both Paragraphs 1 and 2 of Article 7 of the UNCITRAL Conciliation Rules.

Under Paragraph 2, the mediator is also required to take into consideration the nature of the trade and disputes in question and relevant practices, which ensures that the mediator considers the governing law applicable to the dispute as well as fairness and justice.

(2) Paragraph 3

Clarifies that the mediator has discretion to carry out proceedings, such as hearings, in a way that he/she deems appropriate in order to help the parties reach an agreement. [§ UNCITRAL Conciliation Rules Article 7, Paragraph 3]

The IBA Mediation Rules Article 7, Paragraph 3 specifies further details by stating that "Following consultation with the parties, the mediator may take decisions with regard to the procedural conduct of the mediation, including the language(s) of the mediation and the place, the format, times and dates of the mediation sessions." It provides that the mediator can make decisions through consultations with the parties regarding the language(s) to be used for the mediation, place for hearings, method of mediation and time.[22]

In mediation, the decision regarding the place for hearings is important, and most mediation rules require the mediator to make such decisions through consultations with the parties. The UNCITRAL Conciliation Rules also contain the same provision in Article 9, Paragraph 2.[23]

(3) Paragraph 4

Requires the mediator to help the parties to settle the dispute through an agreement for themselves. [§ IBA Mediation Rules Article 8, Paragraph 2]

[22]As the language issue bears a great importance in international mediation, it is separately specified in Article 8 of the B&R Mediation Rules.

[23]UNCITRAL Conciliation Rules Article 9, Paragraph 2: Unless the parties have agreed upon the place where meetings with the conciliator are to be held, such a place will be determined by the conciliator, after consultation with the parties, having regard to the circumstances of the conciliation proceedings.

In addition, the parties are also required to cooperate with the mediator so that the mediation procedures can be conducted in a swift and efficient manner. [§ IBA Mediation Rules Article 7, Paragraph 2] Such an obligation of the parties to cooperate is separately provided in the UNCITRAL Conciliation Rules Article 11.[24]

(4) Paragraph 5

The mediator may request the opinions of experts when the parties agree. This means that the parties and the mediator can consult experts, for example an expert witness, to obtain more accurate information when the dispute at issue is technical and complicated. [IBA Mediation Rules Article 8, paragraph 8] However, further deliberation is needed as to whether expert opinions are really needed in mediation procedures where no clear judgment is expected to be made, unlike in court trials or arbitration.

Article 7 Representation of the Parties

Each party may be represented or assisted by agents, counsel or advocates whose names shall be notified by that party to the mediator.

In mediation procedures, each party is allowed to appoint an attorney-at-law, and so on for its representation, in which case the name of the attorney-at-law, and so on should be notified to the mediator. [§ UNCITRAL Conciliation Rules Article 6, ICSID Conciliation Rules Article 18, Paragraph 1][25]

The type of representation available to each party is not limited to an attorney-at-law; agents, counsels or advocates can act on behalf of the parties in the mediation. There exists the possibility of legal disputes arising due to the differences in attorney-at-law acts of each country regarding the appointment and qualifications of representatives (cf. Article 109 of the Attorney-at-Law Act of R.O. Korea).

The IBA Mediation Rules also contain a provision regarding such representatives in Article 9, Paragraph 2,[26] but do not specify the required qualifications for those representatives.

---

[24]UNCITRAL Conciliation Rules Article 11: The parties will in good faith cooperate with the conciliator and, in particular, will endeavor to comply with requests by the conciliator to submit written materials, provide evidence and attend meetings.

[25]ICSID Conciliation Rules Article 18, Paragraph 1: Each party may be represented or assisted by agents, counsel or advocates whose names and authority shall be notified by that party to the Secretary-General, who shall promptly inform the commission and the other party.

[26]IBA Mediation Rules Article 9, Paragraph 2: During the mediation management conference, each party shall inform the other party and the mediator of the name and contact details of its representative(s) and any other person participating on its behalf in the mediation.

Article 8 Language

The parties may agree on the use of one language to be used in the proceeding. If the parties do not agree on any such procedural language, the official language shall be English.

Multiple countries will participate in the B&R Initiative and any dispute arising therefrom will also involve many countries and enterprises. Therefore, as different languages will be used by them, there exists a high possibility of language issues arising in this international mediation. The parties to the dispute need to agree on a language, and, if they fail to do so, English will be used as an official language (setting a certain time limit will allow for expeditious conduct of the procedures).

Article 9 Conduct of the Mediation

1. The mediation shall be conducted in accordance with the parties' wishes and with the assistance of the mediator.
2. The mediator may communicate with the parties orally or in writing, together or individually, at any point during the mediation. The mediator may conduct meetings with one party only.
3. No information provided orally by a party to the mediator during a separate meeting may be disclosed to any other party by the mediator, unless the party explicitly so authorizes the mediator.
4. In a co-mediation, each co-mediator shall share with the other co-mediator all written or oral communications received from a party or parties. The co-mediators shall coordinate their efforts and jointly conduct the mediation.
5. The mediator may at any time during the proceedings suggest or request that a party provide such additional information or material as the mediator sees fit.

(1) Paragraph 1

Emphasizes that the mediation procedures should, in principle, be carried out based on the parties' autonomy and the mediator should just assist them. [§ IBA Mediation Rules Article 8, Paragraph 1]

(2) Paragraph 2

The mediator is allowed to have a meeting with each party or with all the parties together during the mediation either in writing or orally. Additionally, the mediator can also have a separate meeting with only one party (this paragraph makes it clear that such individual meetings do not harm neutrality). [§ IBA Mediation Rules Article 8, Paragraph 3]

The UNCITRAL Conciliation Rules Article 9, Paragraph 1 also provides that "The conciliator may invite the parties to meet with him or may communicate with them orally or in writing. He may meet or communicate with the parties together or with each of them separately", specifying that the mediator can have a separate meeting with one party as in the IBA Mediation Rules.

(3) Paragraph 3

Emphasizes that information given to the mediator during a separate meeting with one party should not, in principle, be made known to the other party. However, the mediator is allowed to disclose such information with the consent of the first party. [§ IBA Mediation Rules Article 8, Paragraph 4]

The UNCITRAL Conciliation Rules contain a similar provision in Article 10[27] under the title "Disclosure of information". There exist differences between the foregoing article and Article 13 "Confidentiality" of the B&R Mediation Rules regarding whether the information should be disclosed to the other party or a third party. Providing one party's information to the other party can be regarded as "disclosure", while keeping all information related to mediation from a third party "confidentiality".

(4) Paragraph 4

When more than one mediator is participating in mediation, those mediators should share information. Any written or oral information that one of the mediators has obtained should be shared with the other mediator(s). [§ IBA Mediation Rules Article 8, Paragraph 5]

(5) Paragraph 5

Provides that a mediator can request that the parties provide additional materials or information when the mediator considers it necessary. [§ IBA Mediation Rules Article 8, Paragraph 6]

[27]UNCITRAL Conciliation Rules Article 10: When the conciliator receives factual information concerning the dispute from a party, he discloses the substance of that information to the other party in order that the other party may have the opportunity to present any explanation which he considers appropriate. However, when a party gives any information to the conciliator subject to a specific condition that it be kept confidential, the conciliator does not disclose that information to the other party.

Article 10 Settlement

1. Each party may, on his/her own initiative or at the invitation of the mediator, submit to the mediator suggestions for the settlement of the dispute.
2. When it appears to the mediator that there exist elements of a settlement which would be acceptable to the parties, he/she formulates the terms of a possible settlement and submits them to the parties for their observations. After receiving the observations of the parties, the mediator may reformulate the terms of a possible settlement in the light of such observations. However, the mediator shall not have the authority to impose on the parties any partial or complete settlement of the differences or disputes.
3. If the parties reach an agreement on a settlement of the dispute, they draw up and sign a written settlement agreement. If requested by the parties, the mediator draws up, or assists the parties in drawing up, the settlement agreement.
4. The parties by signing the settlement agreement put an end to the dispute and are legally bound by the agreement.
5. If the parties agree to formalize their settlement in an arbitral award for the purpose of enforcement, the mediator(s) conducting his/her/their mediation shall be the arbitrator(s) in expedited arbitration proceedings for that purpose unless otherwise the parties agree.

(1) Paragraph 1

States that each party may present to the mediator suggestions for settlement of disputes through mediation. [§ UNCITRAL Conciliation Rules Article 12]

The IBA Mediation Rules Article 8, Paragraph 7, which states "If requested by the parties, the mediator may make recommendations concerning an appropriate resolution of the differences or disputes", also allows the mediator to present recommendations upon request by the parties.

(2) Paragraph 2

Unlike Paragraph 1, this paragraph provides that the mediator, not the parties, may present recommendations. The mediator can formulate such recommendations as he/she considers appropriate and seek the parties' views on them. He/she can reformulate the recommendations after collecting the parties' opinions.

The mediator has authority to present recommendations, when necessary, to the parties, but he/she should not force the parties to reach an agreement. [§ UNCITRAL Conciliation Rules Article 7, Paragraph 4]

(3) Paragraph 3

Requires that the parties make a written agreement when they agree to settle the dispute, and the mediator can make or help the parties make such a written agreement upon request by the parties. [§ UNCITRAL Conciliation Rules Article 13, Paragraph 2]

(4) Paragraph 4

States explicitly that the mediation procedures are terminated when the parties make a written agreement which binds the parties. The parties are legally bound by the agreement.

(5) Paragraph 5

The parties in dispute may formalize the settlement agreement in an arbitral award through expedited arbitration proceedings to ensure the enforceability of the settlement agreement resulting from mediation. As the New York Convention covers only the awards rendered in *ad hoc* or institutional arbitrations, an arbitration proceeding is necessary for the mediated agreement to be formalized as an arbitral award. In this case, the mediator(s) who conduct(s) the mediation should be the arbitrator(s) in the arbitration proceedings for that purpose unless otherwise the parties agree.

Article 11 Termination of Mediation Proceedings

1. The proceedings are terminated:
   (a) By the signing of the settlement agreement by the parties, on the date of the agreement; or
   (b) By a written declaration of the mediator, after consultation with the parties, to the effect that further efforts at mediation are no longer justified, on the date of the declaration; or
   (c) By a written declaration of one party or the parties addressed to the mediator to the effect that the mediation proceedings are terminated, on the date of the declaration.
2. The declaration of termination shall be made and sent to the Secretary-General of B&R MC without delay. The mediation shall be deemed terminated as of the date of transmission of the declaration to the Secretary-General of B&R MC.

(1) Paragraph 1

The mediation procedures are terminated at the time when the parties to the dispute sign an agreement for the settlement thereof as of the date written in the agreement. [§ UNCITRAL Conciliation Rules Article 15, Subparagraph (a)]

In addition, the mediator can present a written declaration to terminate the procedure when he/she believes that there is no point of continuing the procedures or there is no possibility of the dispute being settled through the agreement of the parties. The procedures are terminated by such a written declaration. [§ UNCITRAL Conciliation Rules Article 15, Subparagraph (b)]

As with a written declaration of the mediator, the mediation procedures are also terminated when a party or the parties to the dispute declare the settlement thereof in writing by agreement, as of the date written in such a declaration. [§ UNCITRAL Conciliation Rules Article 15, Subparagraph (c)]

※ The IBA Mediation Rules Article 11, Paragraph 1[28] also contains a similar provision on the termination of mediation procedures.

(2) Paragraph 2

When the mediation procedures are terminated, the mediator should not delay in notifying the Secretary-General of the B&R MC, and the procedures are considered to be terminated at the time of such notification to the mediation institution. [§ IBA Mediation Rules Article 11, Paragraph 2] (IBA Mediation Rules only provide that the parties should be notified of the termination of the mediation, but it is more desirable that such notification be made to the mediation institution in order that procedures can be followed in a more accurate and efficient manner.)

Article 12 Resort to Arbitral or Judicial Proceedings

The parties undertake not to initiate, during the mediation proceedings, any arbitral or judicial proceedings in respect of a dispute that is the subject of the mediation proceedings, except that a party may initiate arbitral or judicial proceedings where, in his opinion, such proceedings are necessary for preserving his rights.

States that the parties participating in the mediation procedures should not, in principle, resort to arbitral or legal proceedings while the mediation procedures are being continued. However, when a party considers it necessary to do so in order to

[28] IBA Mediation Rules Article 11, Paragraph 1: The mediator shall declare the mediation terminated in writing: (a) upon the signing of a settlement agreement by the parties; (b) upon the withdrawal of any party pursuant to Article 9.4; or (c) if, following consultation with the parties, the mediator determines that the parties will not resolve the differences or disputes through the mediation.

protect his/her own rights, an exception can be made. This shows that having recourse to arbitral or legal proceedings is not always prohibited, and the parties can use their discretion. [§ UNCITRAL Conciliation Rules Article 16]

Therefore, mediation procedures are not always terminated whenever one party initiates legal proceedings, and so on such as a court trial during the mediation procedures (reasons for the termination of mediation procedures are specified in Article 11, Paragraph 1 of the B&R Mediation Rules).

Article 13 Confidentiality

The mediator and the parties must keep confidential all matters relating to the mediation proceedings. Confidentiality extends also to the settlement agreement, except where its disclosure is necessary for purposes of implementation and enforcement.

The parties to the dispute and the mediator are required not to disclose any matters related to mediation procedures, which include a settlement agreement. However, such disclosure is possible when necessary to implement and enforce the settlement agreement. [§ UNCITRAL Conciliation Rules Article 14]

The UNCITRAL Conciliation Rules mentions "confidentiality" rather briefly, while the IBA Mediation Rules Article 10 specifies the issue in great detail under the title of "Privacy and Confidentiality".

Article 14 The Mediator's Role in Other Proceedings

The parties and the mediator undertake that the mediator will not act as an arbitrator or as a representative or counsel of a party in any arbitral or judicial proceedings in respect of a dispute that is the subject of the mediation proceedings. The parties also undertake that they will not present the mediator as a witness in any such proceedings.

The parties and mediator should make sure that, if the dispute for which mediation procedures have commenced is submitted for arbitration or trials, the same mediator is not allowed to serve as an arbitrator or representative. In addition, the parties should not have the mediator become a witness in such legal proceedings. [§ UNCITRAL Conciliation Rules Article 19]

This paragraph is designed to prevent a situation where, if the mediator could be designated as an arbitrator for arbitration following the termination of mediation, the parties would be reluctant to disclose more information or facts during the mediation, making the mediation procedures difficult. Furthermore, this paragraph is also aimed at preventing any unfair situation where a mediator who learned of confidential matters and facts during mediation procedures acts as an agent for the other party in trials.

In addition, having the mediator become a witness in arbitration or trials after the termination of mediation procedures is also prohibited as it will put a significantly unfair burden on him/her.

Article 15 Admissibility of Evidence in Other Proceedings

The parties undertake not to rely on, or introduce as evidence in arbitral or judicial proceedings, whether or not such proceedings relate to the dispute that is the subject of the mediation proceedings, any of the following:

(a) Views expressed or suggestions made by the other party in respect of a possible settlement of the dispute;
(b) Admissions made by the other party in the course of the mediation proceedings;
(c) Proposals made by the mediator;
(d) The fact that the other party has indicated his/her willingness to accept a proposal for settlement made by the mediator.

If any evidence presented during the mediation procedures was also available for arbitration or trials, the parties would not disclose much of the evidence during the mediation procedures, which could be an obstacle to the procedures being carried out smoothly. Each party is also prohibited from using any evidence presented in the mediation procedures for arbitration or trials since doing so would put the other party at a disadvantage. [§ UNCITRAL Conciliation Rules Article 20]

Such evidence prevented from being used for arbitration or trials includes opinions of a party submitted to the other party for the settlement of the dispute, admissions made by the other party regarding the dispute, and proposals of the mediator.

Article 16 Costs

1. Before the commencement of the mediation proceedings, the Secretariat shall provide the parties with the information about the proposed costs. Upon the termination of the mediation proceedings, the Secretary-General fixes the costs of the mediation and gives a written notice thereof to the parties. The term "costs" includes only:

   (a) The fee of the mediator which shall be reasonable in amount and the travel and other expenses of the mediator;
   (b) The administrative expenses of the B&R MC;
   (c) The travel and other expenses of witnesses requested by the mediator with the consent of the parties;
   (d) The cost of any expert advice requested by the mediator with the consent of the parties.

2. The costs, as defined above, are borne equally by the parties unless the settlement agreement provides for a different apportionment. All other expenses incurred by a party are borne by that party.
3. The Secretary-General of the B&R MC may request each party to deposit an equal amount as an advance for the costs and expenses.

(1) Paragraph 1

Before the commencement of the mediation proceedings, the Secretariat should provide the parties with the information about the fees and expenses of mediation. The Secretariat should maintain the standard list of fee and expenses which may be varied depending on mediators. Upon the termination of the proceedings, the Secretary-General should fix the costs and give a written notice of costs to the parties in dispute.

The costs of mediation should, in principle, be borne by the parties, which the mediator confirms and sends notice of to the parties. [§ UNCITRAL Conciliation Rules Article 17, Paragraph 1]

Such costs include (a) reasonable fees for the mediator and travel and other expenses spent by the mediator for the mediation, (b) expenses spent on the administration of the B&R MC, (c) travel and other expenses of witnesses designated by the mediator upon the agreement of the parties, and (d) costs of experts whom the mediator consulted upon the agreement of the parties. (In the UNCITRAL Conciliation Rules, which envisage *ad hoc* mediation, there is no provision regarding administrative expenses of the mediation institution.)

(2) Paragraph 2

In principle, the parties bear all costs of mediation in equal shares unless otherwise agreed by the parties. Other expenses spent by a party should be borne by that party. [§ UNCITRAL Conciliation Rules Article 17, Paragraph 2]

(3) Paragraph 3

Costs for mediation, such as fees of the mediator, should be deposited in the mediation institution in advance.

The UNCITRAL Conciliation Rules Article 18, Paragraph 1 allows the mediator to request that mediation costs be deposited, while in mediation administered by the B&R MC, the mediation center may request that the parties deposit such expenses.

Appendix 5
Dispute Resolution Mechanism for the Belt and Road

Rajesh Sharma

A. **Background**

The Belt and Road (B&R) Initiative involves infrastructure development in the countries along the Belt and Road. Some of those projects may involve more than one country along the Belt and Road. It may be too complicated and time-consuming to negotiate bilateral or multilateral FTAs which will delay the execution of infrastructure projects. Timely completion of roads, bridges, railway lines and power projects will bring benefits to the people down in line immediately as compared to the flow of benefits originating from any FTA. The project which helps or touches people at large will also be widely accepted as compared to FTAs which are generally resisted by people.

On a technical level FTAs are not liberal enough to achieve the fullest level of benefits such as free movements of capital, technology and professionals both of high skills and low skills. Therefore, it is important that the B&R Initiative, instead of reaching a grand FTA or several FTAs, should aim at project-by-project cooperation along the Belt and Road. This approach will help timely completion of projects and for a short period of time countries involved in any project will be open to accept freedom of movement of capital, technology and people. Once the project finishes, the level and scope of cooperation could be modified. With completion of projects, people in the area or country will see the direct and immediate benefits of B&R. One successful project will lead to another success and over the period with the confidence and trust among the countries on the Belt and Road, a grand FTA will be achieved.

Though project-by-project negotiation may be able to complete the project on time and bring the benefits to the people on ground but it is also true that such projects may also lead to dispute among private parties, private parties with governments and between governments too. It is also possible that one action or decision may give rise to disputes based on contract, treaty or other instruments, which may involve private parties and governments. It is also important that while dispute is being resolved the project must go on so that it can be completed on time,

© Zhejiang University Press 2020

G. Wang et al., *Dispute Resolution Mechanism for the Belt and Road Initiative*,
https://doi.org/10.1007/978-981-15-1975-8

results could be seen and benefits could flow from that project immediately. For example, a payment dispute for a section of road project should not hinder the completion of the full road.

Therefore, it is proposed that for the B&R a dispute resolution mechanism should be designed to deal with the disputes arising out of or related to a particular project.

Such disputes may involve contractual disputes among private parties, private parties and a government, investment disputes, or a nullification and impairment (mainly happens in FTA or Trade Agreements) types of disputes among two or more governments. The contractual disputes may involve main contractors, and even sub-contractors. In this regard there are a few options to be considered:

Option 1 One Tribunal for all Disputes

In B&R dispute resolution mechanism it is possible to use one tribunal to resolve all kinds of disputes: contractual, investment and nullification and impairment disputes. It is useful if one action gives rise to all kinds of disputes. In that situation, the tribunal may deal with issues and related parties at a time and apply the relevant law in that particular issue. For example, contractual disputes can be resolved among private parties. If that dispute involves investment disputes then that private party and the relevant government may resolve that investment dispute before the same tribunal. In that case the other private party may not be involved.

If the relevant action of a government has caused any nullification or impairment, then the same tribunal can resolve that dispute between two governments and at that time private parties may not take part. It is also possible that all the parties may be present and take part if a dispute involves all kinds of disputes.

> **Benefits**: One stop service, saving time and cost, and avoiding duplication of processes.
> **Risks**: In some cases such as the state–state dispute, private parties may get involved.

Option 2 Different Tribunals for Different Disputes

This is a current prevailing practice. Commercial disputes go for arbitration, investment disputes go for investment arbitration and nullification and impairment dispute go for a different (FTA) tribunal.

> **Benefits**: Separate disputes will be dealt with separately.
> **Risks**: Time-consuming, costly, duplication of processes and that the same parties may use the same dispute type in two different forums, such as contractual dispute and investment dispute, investment dispute and nullification and impairment dispute.

Stages/Processes of Dispute Resolution

All the countries along the Belt and Road are supporters of an amicable solution of any dispute. Therefore, the dispute resolution mechanism for B&R should give emphasis to consultation/negotiation and mediation as the main method of resolving disputes. At the same time, the dispute resolution mechanism should also be able to deal with disputes which cannot be resolved through consultations and/or mediation. In those cases, the dispute resolution framework should have a rule-based final and binding determination, which satisfies the test of efficiency, effectiveness, transparency and practicality.

Agreed Stages of Dispute Resolution

Stage 1: Consultations/Negotiation
Stage 2: Mediation (if consultation fails or any issue is not resolved through consultation)
Stage 3: Arbitration (if mediation fails or any issue is not resolved through mediation)
Stage 4: Execution

(i) Execution of the agreement reached at the consultation stage;
(ii) Execution of the agreement reached at mediation stage;
(iii) Enforcement of the arbitration award/panel report.

Issues to Be Considered Further

1. It is agreed that consultation, then mediation, and then arbitration will be followed. However, it is to be considered further if the responding party does not take part in consultation, then whether the complaining party should still follow the next stage of mediation or may go directly to arbitration.
2. If the parties are required to follow each stage, then is it necessary to wait till the end of the period of consultation (e.g. 60 days) to move to mediation or wait till the end of the mediation (e.g. 60 days) to move to arbitration, or in the situation when the responding party has indicated its intention of not following the process then would it be possible for the complainant to move directly to the next step or to arbitration?
3. Should Consultation–Mediation–Arbitration be followed as a one way street or is it possible to shift back and forth or combine two processes (mainly mediation and arbitration) or even if mediation is successful, still use arbitration to ensure execution of the settlement agreement as an award both locally and internationally (considering that there is not legal mechanism to enforce the mediation agreement as such across the border)?

Scope/Coverage/Types of Dispute

Whether the dispute settlement mechanism is separate for separate disputes (e.g. commercial arbitration, investment dispute and nullification and impairment dispute) or one stop system, it is important to decide the scope/coverage/types of dispute which could be resolved under the proposed mechanism. For example:

Contractual Dispute: Including sub-contracts, payment, wages relating to infrastructure/projects.

Investment Dispute: Should/should not include the current BITs. It can include the disputes on investment provisions which might be agreed for B&R. Or parties agree to treat infrastructure disputes as investment disputes in their relevant contract to grant tribunal under B&R the required jurisdiction.

Nullification or Impairment Dispute: For future provisions to be agreed under B&R. Or through the infrastructure contract/or MOU agreed by governments without encroaching upon the scope of the current FTAs signed by countries along the Belt and Road or the WTO.

For such disputes, generally the government measures are challenged, so in this regard it is important to agree:

- **Measures which are effective**;
- **Measures which are proposed** (for consultation stage and/or mediation stage);
- **Measures which are passed/adopted by a government but not in operation yet**;
- **Measures of federal level/state level/local level or any level** (it is to note some FTAs do not include measures taken by local governments).

Advance Ruling: Parties may get a ruling through this mechanism which will be effective during the construction or operation of any project. It will be helpful in transfer of equipment need for the construction or operation or project, exempt from duties of the host or other involved countries on the Belt and Road, and issues relating to Rules of Origin. This system can also be used for the measures which have been adopted but not implemented. This can be used as a stabilization clause for the purpose of investment disputes. Advance ruling may be issued by the relevant administrative body, such as customs and tax, but the dispute settlement system of B&R can be used if there is a dispute on the decision of the government authorities or measures are at the proposal stage or waiting for the implementation or execution. In investment cases it may serve as a stabilization clause so that the host government may not be able to apply new rules on a particular project while the government will have enough regulatory space for its functioning.

This system can be used through the panel/arbitration process.

Advisory Opinion: The dispute settlement mechanism may be used for advisory opinion on proposed measures, or measures which have been passed/adopted but not implemented. This method can work together with the advance ruling system or as an alternative. This is also good for preventing any issue to reach to the level of dispute. Those countries, which have low levels of capacity along the Belt and Road, may get benefit from this system.

Cooperation

A new trend has emerged in the dispute settlement mechanism under FTAs which expects parties to a dispute to cooperate in finding solutions to the dispute. Therefore, the following issues need to be agreed:

1. Should there be a provision of cooperation in the dispute settlement mechanism of B&R?
2. If yes, then should it be simply aspirational?
3. Or should it be a general obligation without any consequence?
4. Or should it be an obligation under the dispute settlement running through every stage of the process and breach of which may result into certain consequences?

For example, if the responding party does not take part in consultation, should it be considered as the breach of the cooperation provision? Such non-cooperation can be used for drawing negative inference if the responding party challenges/objects/appeals the award. Similarly, if the responding party does not pay damages or executes award then it may be a breach of the non-cooperation provision.

Confidential or Transparent Dispute Settlement Process

Option 1

As a matter of principle, it is important to decide whether the dispute settlement mechanism under B&R should be totally confidential, or partially confidential, or wholly or partly transparent.

Option 2

It is also possible to make consultation and mediation process confidential and keep the arbitration process transparent.

Option 3

The third option is to make all stages of dispute settlement transparent particularly when one party is a government in commercial arbitration, investment arbitration and dispute on nullification and impairment.

B. **Consultation**

Consultations should be the first stage of the dispute settlement mechanism.

Upon receiving the request for consultations, the party complained against should first acknowledge the receipt of the request promptly within a specified period of time. Thereafter, the parties should enter into consultations within a specified time and consult in good faith with a view to reaching a mutual agreement within a specified time period.

The time period should be counted from the date of issuing the notice as it will be difficult to ascertain the date of receiving the notice. It is possible to create a deemed date of receipt (1–2 days after sending the notice) if the notice is sent by electronic means such as e-mail. If a dispute settlement secretariat is established under B&R then the date of receipt will be the date of receipt by the secretariat.

In the written request for consultations, the facts, relevant provisions of the agreement and legal reasoning behind the complaint must be communicated to the party complained against clearly so that consultations may be conducted in an effective and efficient manner.

It is suggested that the relevant government personnel should be available when needed during consultations.

To deal with cases of urgency, there should be an expedited process of consultations.

Modes of Consultations

With a view to conducting consultations effectively and efficiently, parties should be allowed to conduct consultations in person or by alternative means using telecommunications, video-conferencing and other similar modes of communications.

This approach will save time, cost and will increase efficiency.

Venue of Consultations

If consultations are held in person, the parties may agree to a place for consultations.

If possible, it should be close to the place/country of the infrastructure project which may be the subject of the dispute.

If no agreement is reached, as a default, the place of the party complained against should be the place for consultations.

Face-to-face consultations may be substituted or mixed with consultations via video-conferencing, tele-communication, Skype and so on. It will be useful for the multiparty consultations.

Time Period for Consultations

To start, a shorter period of time for the acknowledgment of the request for consultations should be provided as it is a mere act to inform the complaining party that the party complained against has received the request.

The time period should be counted from the date of issuing of the notice as it will be difficult to ascertain the date of receiving the notice. It is possible to create a deemed date of receipt (1–2 days after sending the notice) if the notice is sent by electronic means such as e-mail.

If a dispute resolution secretariat is established under B&R then the date of receipt will be the date of receipt by the secretariat.

Therefore, the time for acknowledging the request for consultations should be from 3 to 5 days maximum. Parties should be encouraged to send the acknowledgment immediately after receiving the request for consultations.

The date of acknowledgment may serve as the date of the receipt of the request for consultations.

It is suggested that a maximum period of 10 days should be given as a period to reply to the request for consultations. The starting date for the calculation of any time period should be counted from the date of acknowledgment of the request for consultations, or from the date of receipt or date of issuing of the notice as the case may be.

In order to give consultations a full opportunity to succeed, the B&R dispute resolution mechanism should provide 60 days for consultations. With the agreement of the parties, the period may be extended mainly when there is a possibility of resolution of the dispute.

With a view to reaching a mutually agreed solution as quickly as possible, in cases of urgency, a short period of 20 days for consultations should be allowed. It is possible to identify a few situations which warrant expedited consultations, such as perishable goods, design related issues, urgent and important change in structure and so on.

Rights of the Parties in Further Proceedings

The consultation process should not be prejudicial to the rights of the parties in later or other proceedings of the B&R dispute resolution.

C. Mediation

Please see the policy paper by Professor Park, et al.

D. Arbitration

Arbitration is the third stage of the dispute settlement process in B&R.

However, when the responding party does not participate, the complaining party should have a choice to go directly to the arbitration stage.

For the purposes of clarity, only the complaining party who initiated the consultation process should be allowed to make the request for the establishment of an arbitral panel. Therefore, language like "any party" should be avoided. It is highly unlikely that after consultation the responding party may discover any cause of action. Even if this is the case it can be sorted out through counterclaim filed by the responding party.

To make the process of dispute resolution simpler and without incurring any recurring costs of implementation, it is suggested that the request to establish an arbitral panel be sent by the complaining party to the party complained against directly if there is no secretariat of dispute settlement.

In other words, if there is an institution under B&R to deal with disputes, then the notice of arbitration and other exchange of documents should be conducted through the secretariat.

It is suggested that for the purpose of initiating the arbitral process, the complaining party should be simply required to send a request for the establishment of an arbitration panel and make reference to the content sent for the consultations process, that is, the factual and legal basis of the claim. Only when new facts, evidence or issues emerge in relation to the issues which were under consultation, mediation and now subject to arbitration, should the factual and legal basis in support of arbitration claim be submitted.

Composition of the Arbitral Tribunal

The number of arbitrators shall be one/three. For a simple case, sole arbitrator should be appointed. It will save time and cost and most importantly resolve the dispute quickly so that infrastructure projects could be completed in time.

In order to make the process efficient, the complaining party should nominate its arbitrator together with the request for the establishment of an arbitral panel. In this way the process of appointment of arbitrator can be expedited.

As a default rule, a provision for an arbitral tribunal to consist of a sole arbitrator should be included, in situations where the party complained against fails to appoint its arbitrator within the specified time.

To expedite the process of arbitration, a total of 15 days should be given to the responding party to nominate its arbitrator and such a time period should be counted from the date of the request for the establishment of an arbitral tribunal.

B&R dispute resolution should follow Indicative List of Arbitrators and Indicative List of Chair. For the purpose of parties appointed arbitrator there should be flexibility in appointing an arbitrator. Particularly a private party should have an option to choose an arbitrator from the indicative list of his country as well as any other person it deems fit for the particular dispute.

There should be provisions to deal with the appointment of the substitute arbitrators. The process of appointment of the substitute arbitrators should be the same as that adopted for the appointment of the arbitrator who is going to be replaced.

In that regard, the standard process of appointment should first be used, failing which the default process can be used.

As a default process the arbitrators or chairman should be appointed on the lottery system. For this, names will be selected from the Indicative List of Arbitrators and the Indicative List of Chair.

If a dispute resolution secretariat is established, then the secretariat may appoint the arbitrators or chairman with an option given to the parties to reject names of the arbitrators or the chairman.

There is no need to involve DG of the WTO or any independent party to select arbitrators and/or the chairman.

Qualification of Arbitrators and the Chair

The B&R dispute resolution mechanism should follow the universal professional qualifications, that is every member of the tribunal including the chair must have expertise, or experience in law, international trade or other matters covered by the contract, investment or treaty or resolution of disputes arising under international trade agreements.

Personal qualities of the arbitrators, that is, objectivity, reliability and sound judgment, should be added as one of the qualification requirements for the arbitrators.

It is also suggested that the WTO Rules of Conduct for the Understanding on Rules and Procedures Governing the Settlement of Disputes (WT/DSB/RC/1) should be included particularly for nullification and impairment disputes.

In order to clarify the basic rule, it may also be added that the tribunal must remain independent and impartial throughout the arbitral proceedings as one of the qualifications.

The restriction on nationality, employment, usual place of residence and the involvement in the dispute of the chair should also be incorporated to maintain the integrity of the process. It is important to add explanation with regards to nationality, such as dual nationality.

It should be clarified that the general restrictions on the chair are not applicable in a situation where a sole arbitrator is appointed as default.

For specialized dispute such as the construction dispute, investment dispute, maritime dispute, IP dispute, and various specific types of dispute in trade agreements, a qualification related to that specific knowledge may be required from the parties appointing the arbitrators or the chairman.

Functions of the Arbitral Tribunal

The tribunal shall decide the case by analyzing the facts and law objectively.

For treaties and government level contracts, the VCLT as a tool for interpretation should be included.

In nullification and impairment, the arbitral tribunal must have power to declare a measure inconsistent with the agreement and to recommend the party complained against to remove such inconsistency.

In the commercial arbitration, the tribunal should award compensation.

In the investment arbitration, the tribunal should be able to award compensation as well as give recommendation for amendment or suggestions to make the measure consistent with the investment policy.

Although the arbitral tribunal's suggestions as how to remove the inconsistency are dependent on the terms of reference, such suggestions should be included as part of the tribunal's report without any reference to terms of reference. Alternatively, the terms of reference must always include the requirement for suggestions as to how to remove inconsistency.

While dealing with the nullification and impairment dispute, the arbitral tribunal cannot add to or diminish any rights or obligations of parties granted in the agreement.

In order to deal with such a situation, there should be a provision which authorizes the parties to treat that part of the arbitral tribunal's decision as invalid if both parties agree that that part of the decision of the tribunal has gone beyond the intention of the parties in the agreement.

In order to make this process even more institutional, a body like the joint committee should be established which should have power to override the decision of the arbitral tribunal where both parties agree that the decision of the arbitral tribunal is inconsistent with their intention in the agreement.

Otherwise, the decision of the arbitral tribunal shall be final and binding on the parties.

Terms of Reference

In addition to the general terms of reference, that is, to examine, to determine and to recommend, there should be requirement on the arbitral tribunal to give reasons for its decision, its conclusion on the nullification and impairment of benefits and suggestions as to how to implement the recommendations.

It is advisable to start counting the time period for the issuance of the terms of reference from the date of the composition of the tribunal instead of the date of the issuance of the request for the arbitration.

Hearings

To make the dispute settlement mechanism more efficient, the parties should be allowed to meet the tribunal soon after its composition as part of the preliminary meeting.

Therefore, a short period of time such as 10 days from the date of composition of the tribunal for the preliminary meeting with the parties to agree on the issues in conflict.

This preliminary meeting may be conducted in person or via video-conferencing or teleconferencing.

The chairman may conduct, on behalf of the tribunal, the preliminary meeting with the parties.

As a basic principle, parties should get at least one but no more than two rights of presentation before the tribunal.

As the complaining party initiates the arbitral proceedings, so the complaining party should get the first opportunity to present its case.

The party complained against should get the opportunity to respond to the arguments made by the complaining party.

In order to complete the presentation, the parties should be allowed to make a rebuttal and surrebuttal after the substantive arguments.

As questions from the arbitral tribunal are important for arriving at its decision, the tribunal should have power to ask oral and written questions from the parties, before, during or after substantive arguments. Oral questions may be answered orally and the written questions should be answered in writing.

Parties should be able to submit for initial written submissions of arguments on the issues in dispute.

The time period for oral presentation, rebuttal and surrebuttal should be left to the parties and the tribunal to agree upon. Any agreement or decision on time period should be guided by the principle of efficiency of the process.

It should be ensured that the parties get enough time to present their case adequately, in line with the principles of natural justice.

The working language of the arbitration should be English unless the parties agree otherwise. Any use of other languages should be agreed in the light of the efficiency of the process including the linguistic ability of the tribunal.

If the tribunal is a regular tribunal of three members, a party should submit four sets of copies of any document and if the tribunal consists of a sole arbitrator, any document should be submitted in two sets of copies as a default rule.

For the purpose of calculating the time period, the starting date should be the next day of the occurrence of an event or any specified date.

Therefore, if the last date falls on a holiday in the country or place of arbitration which is required to submit a document, then as a default the next working day should be the last day, irrespective of whether or not that day is a holiday in the other country.

The parties should allow to agree on the date and time of hearings in consultation with the chairman and the other panel members. In this regard, attention should be paid to the urgency of the matter.

The parties should agree on the place of hearing.

While suggesting the respondent's territory as the place of hearing as the default rule, it may be agreed that the capital city of that place to be the exact place of hearing. At the same time, taking into account the convenience of the panel members, experts and witnesses, location of the infrastructure projects, the parties and the arbitral tribunal, there should be an option to choose a third place as the place of hearing.

As a default rule, the respondent is fully responsible for the costs if the place of hearing is in the respondent's territory. At the same time, the parties to share the costs of the hearing if the place of hearing is selected by the mutual agreement of the parties or such a place is a third country as a default.

Technical Experts and Information

The arbitration tribunal should be allowed to use experts in assisting the tribunal in the dispute settlement procedure.

The tribunal on its own or with the assistance of the parties may decide to engage an expert whenever necessary.

The tribunal should be authorized to select the technical experts. As far as possible, such technical experts must not be from disputing parties' country though the countries involved in dispute may give their views. Only in the circumstances where an expert on a certain technical issue is not available outside the country of disputing parties may the expert from the country of disputing parties be invited.

The time period to submit the technical advice or expert report should be kept to a minimum in order to make the dispute settlement system more efficient.

The expert report should be submitted in writing to the arbitral tribunal and the copy of the same should be given to each of the parties.

Upon receiving the expert report, the parties should be given adequate opportunities to comment on the technical report, and the parties may submit their comments in writing.

If the tribunal relies on the expert report in deciding the case, it must also take into account the comments provided by the parties.

The experts may also assist the arbitral tribunal by being present during the hearing. However, experts are not allowed to take part in the deliberations of the tribunal and in the decision-making process.

Multiple Disputes, Multiple Parties, Consolidation

There should be the provision of consolidation of multiple claims, multiple disputes and multiple parties.

For this purpose, the principle of international commercial arbitration should be borrowed.

There should be a provision for allowing counterclaim not only in the commercial arbitration but also in investment claims.

Interim Order, Emergency Order, Directions

The tribunal should have power to grant interim order or issue appropriate directions.

If such orders are of urgent nature then there should be the provision of the emergency arbitrator.

However, such decisions or orders should not be issued ex parte. The responding parties should be given the right to present its argument before such orders or awards are issued.

Arbitral Award/Report/Decision/Order

There should be two-stage processes: the system of the initial and the final report.

The report/award should be in three parts: The first part should be the facts and arguments of the parties, the second part should be the reasoning of the tribunal and the third part should be the conclusion of the tribunal including any recommendations or suggestions as to how to bring the impugned measure in line with the agreement (in case of nullification and impairment disputes as well as investment disputes).

Initial report/award should consist of facts and arguments of the parties.

The final report/award should consist of, in addition to facts and arguments, reasoning of the tribunal and recommendations, suggestion or order of the tribunal.

The initial report should be issued within 60 days from the date of composition of the tribunal.

In cases of urgency, the initial report should be issued in 30 days from the date of the composition of the arbitral tribunal. This will be in line with an efficient system of dispute settlement.

If the tribunal needs an extra period of time to issue the initial report, an additional maximum period of 20 days should be set for issuing the initial report.

Moreover, the tribunal should give its reason for the delay or any extension of time and the estimated period for the release of the initial report in writing to the parties. In cases of urgency including perishable goods, the maximum additional period of time should only be 10 days from the end of the prescribed period of 30 days from the date of the composition of the tribunal.

The practice of providing a lump-sum period for everything is neither efficient nor effective; therefore, such an approach should not be followed.

The parties should be given 10 days from the issuance of the initial report to make any comments on the initial report.

The tribunal should pay due regard to the comments made by the parties or make further examination if appropriate. As a matter of fairness and for reasons of transparency, the final report should include the comments of the parties on the initial reports.

The final report should be issued 30 days after the issuance of the initial report.

Following the general practice, it should be ensured that the decision by the tribunal is made by consensus as far as possible. When there is no consensus, the majority rule should be applied. The final report should include both majority and minority opinion but the names of the panel members with majority or minority views must be anonymous.

Following the principle of transparency (where applicable), the final report should be made public in 10 days from the date of its issuance of the final report to the parties.

Implementation of the Arbitral Award, Report, Decision

As a general principle, the arbitral report/award is final and binding and the responding party has obligations to follow the recommendations of the tribunal immediately or within a reasonable time period.

Commercial arbitral awards and investment awards should be enforced under the New York Convention.

Therefore, it should be made sure that the place of arbitration is in the New York Convention country (selected along the Belt and Road). If the responding party is from the non-signatory of the New York Convention, then first it should be encouraged to sign the New York Convention. In the mean time, to ensure effectiveness of enforcement a system of "security" for cost or damages may be considered.

For the execution of award under B&R dispute resolution mechanism, state should not be allowed to raise the defense of sovereign immunity, in order to ensure that a separate agreement or declaration must be signed by the state before the commencement of arbitration.

Alternatively, the dispute resolution clause in a contract or in a treaty or in the dispute settlement mechanism of B&R should declare that the agreement to arbitrate should be treated as the waiver of immunity at the time of execution of award.

In order to make the dispute settlement system efficient and effective, parties should be given only 20 days from the issuance of the final report/award to agree on the reasonable period of time for the execution of the award.

If the parties do not agree on the reasonable period of time, the matter should be referred to the original arbitral panel/mediation as far as possible. For a speedy resolution, only 15 days should be given to the tribunal to determine the reasonable period of time and for that purpose, even a single panel member may constitute the panel.

Consequences of Non-implementation of the Arbitral Report/Award

Full and immediate implementation of the arbitral report/award should be adopted as the general principle and the primary obligation of the responding party. The system of compensation and suspension of benefits should be a temporary recourse until the responding party eliminates the inconsistent measures particularly in nullification and impairment disputes. This system can be extended in investment disputes too.

While deciding whether to seek compensation or initiate the suspension of benefits by the complaining party, regard must be paid to the good faith attempt made by the responding party.

The arbitral tribunal/mediator/conciliator should also give weight to the good faith attempt of the responding party while deciding the level of compensation or the level of suspension of benefits.

If the responding party needs to extend the reasonable period of time, it should make such a request 20 days before the expiry of the reasonable period of time.

However, only one extension of time period should be allowed provided such a request is made 20 days before the expiration of the reasonable period of time together with an implementation plan as to how the responding party is going to eliminate the inconsistent measure or execute the award in full.

Both the complaining party and the responding party may initiate the request for negotiation for compensation.

The parties should have 20 days to agree on the level of compensation.

A sole arbitrator or a mediator should be used to decide the level of compensation to maintain the efficiency of the dispute resolution mechanism.

The arbitral tribunal should be required to give its decision (or the parties should agree in mediation) on the level of compensation within 20 days from the date of referral of the matter to the arbitral tribunal consisting of a sole arbitrator or the original three members or through mediation.

If the responding party has taken any steps toward implementation, those efforts should be taken into account while determining the level of compensation by the arbitral tribunal/or through mediation.

The arbitral tribunal, after deciding the level of compensation, may also decide or recommend a plan for payment in phases because once the inconsistency is eliminated, the responding party can stop making any compensatory payments. Such an arrangement may also be reached among the parties through mediation.

In the spirit of cooperation and good faith, the complaining party may not demand for any compensation, or agree to a lower level of compensation or forgo any agreed amount of compensation.

The process of suspension of benefits should not commence just because the parties failed to reach any agreement on the level of compensation within the prescribed time period, unless the responding party is not acting in good faith.

The amount of compensation may be paid in US dollars or in any other agreed currency. The money will be kept in a trust account so that the money could be used for assisting the responding party in implementing the award/report mainly for making measures in line with the recommendations. The money can be used for the capacity building and general welfare of the community or the local area where the infrastructure projects are carried on.

Suspension of Benefits

The suspension of benefits may be triggered in three situations. First, after the issuance of the final report, where the responding party shows no intention to comply with the recommendations in the report, the complaining party may start the process of suspending the benefits accruing to the responding party.

Since it has been proposed that after the breakdown of the negotiations on compensation, the matter should be referred to the arbitral tribunal/mediation for determination, a mere failure to agree on the level of compensation may not be a logical ground for commencing the procedure of the suspension of benefits.

Secondly, the suspension of benefits should be allowed when the responding party does not request for any extension of time after the end of the reasonable period of time and shows lack of good faith by not taking any steps toward implementation during the reasonable period of time.

The third situation where the complaining party may initiate the process of the suspension of benefits is when both parties agree to the amount of compensation together or in mediation or it is determined by the tribunal but the responding party does not make the payment as per the payment plan.

In the spirit of cooperation, a default or delay in part of the compensation should not result in the harsh situation of suspension of benefits, which is the highest form of retaliatory measure against the responding party.

Before the suspension of benefits, the complaining party should give a written notice to the responding party which contains the proposed level of suspension of benefits, affected sector or sectors and the proposed date of commencement of the suspension. In general, the notice period is for 30 days; however, to keep the system efficient and effective, the notice period should provide for 20 days of time. At the same time, the complaining party should also refer the matter to the original arbitral panel for its approval on the proposed plan on the suspension of benefits or initiate mediation to reach an agreement among the parties.

Therefore, the proposed combined process of notice and approval at the same time will make the system efficient and effective. However, the suspension of benefits will not be operative either during the notice period or during the determination of the matter by the arbitral tribunal.

The suspension of benefits must follow the general principles which are: First, when considering what benefits to suspend, the complaining party should first seek to suspend benefits in the same sector or sectors as those are affected by the impugned measures. If the complaining party considers that it is not practicable or effective to suspend benefits in the same sector, it may suspend benefits in other sectors. An example or clarification should be provided as to a similar sector particularly in services, and IP areas. Denial of benefits in the investment arbitration may be considered as cross-retaliation.

The second general principle is that the benefits, which are going to be suspended, must arise out of the relevant agreement.

The third general principle is that the suspension of benefits is a temporary measure which must be lifted once the responding party fully complies with the recommendations in the final report.

The principle that the suspension of benefits cannot substitute full implementation should also be emphasized.

The original arbitral tribunal or a sole arbitrator chosen from the original panel should conduct the compliance review. Or the parties may agree to use mediation to resolve the dispute relating to the compliance review. To complete the compliance review, the tribunal should take the same time as that taken for the determination of compensation or level of the suspension of benefits, that is, 20 days from the referral of the issue.

To maintain the efficiency of the system, a maximum of 15 days of additional time period should be provided to the tribunal to complete the compliance review.

E. **Appeal Mechanism**

Please see the policy paper by Ambassador Supperamanian

- Nullification and Impairment Disputes, and;
- Investment Disputes.

F. **Other Issues**

Capacity-Building Initiatives

As the countries along the Belt and Road are at a stage of different levels of development, it is important that B&R should help those disadvantageous countries through capacity-building programs. Those programs may include developing a modern dispute resolution system so that the countries may propose a capable and qualified arbitrator, or mediator for their indicative list of dispute resolvers. If a country has not signed the New York Convention then assistance could be provided for signature and ratification, training on investment-related disputes and commercial disputes. Initially, it may need funding to run the program but with such initiatives future disputes can be avoided which will save huge money and time. As proposed earlier, any compensation paid by a country may be used for the development of that country later in terms of aid for trade, capacity-building training in teaching a training of trade, investment and dispute resolution.

Legal Aid/Advisory Services

Following the success of Advisory Center of the WTO, B&R should also consider establishing a legal and technical advisory center or aid service center. This center will help the parties to understand their rights and obligations. It will create fairness in the execution of projects under B&R. Small economies, small enterprises and economically disadvantageous parties will feel secured and protected against big parties.

Dispute Resolution Center/Secretariat

To provide one stop service and to deal with disputes relating to multiple projects and multiple parties, it is important that a small secretariat or Dispute Resolution Center of B&R should be established. It will provide systemic and coordinated support in resolution of disputes. Such a Center or secretariat may also provide support for the *ad hoc* or regular appeal system. Having all information at one place or managed through one system may help parties and increase efficiency and effectiveness. With the centralized information, it will be possible to make a decision or planning for the consolidation or disputes on the same subject matter, appointment of mediators, arbitrators and chairmen, follow up in execution of award, report and settlement agreement. It will involve costs but with few big problems, it could be managed efficiently and effectively.

The members are invited to give their comments, suggestions and consent on the principles presented here.

Once the broad principles are agreed, then the language of the provisions can be drafted accordingly.

Appendix 6
The Belt and Road Resolution of Disputes: Establishment of an Appellate Mechanism

Supperamanian Manickham

The Belt and Road Framework of Cooperation will lead to the exponential increase in regional trade and economic activities. This will create the corresponding need to manage the inevitable increase in the number of international disputes. Currently, there are various approaches to resolve disputes. The purpose of this paper is to explore the desirability and feasibility of establishing an appellate mechanism as an additional facility for the arbitration system.

It must be acknowledged that the region is witnessing a proliferation of arbitration cases under sophisticated institutions and rules for arbitration. International arbitration is being recognized as an effective mode of dispute resolution.

Over the last two decades, arbitration has undoubtedly become the most popular alternative to litigation in many parts of the world. It's a buzzword of speed, confidentiality and ease of enforcement that made it especially popular among international businesses.

However, the arbitration is not perfect, and users have quite frequently reported a less rosy picture. The arbitral tribunals' lack of policy powers and its fear of being accused of procedural unfairness leave the arbitral process prone to delay, and dilatory tactics translating to increased time and cost. In some cases, the scarcity of experienced arbitrators presents real problems in ensuring fair and effective procedures.

Arbitration of investment disputes, in particular, has been subject to close scrutiny and strong criticisms in view of its own set of limitations. The last decade has witnessed an unprecedented increase in the use of investor-state arbitration highlighting numerous shortcomings of the existing investor-state dispute settlement systems. The increased litigation has led to both the process and the outcome being questioned, and this has undermined the growth of a harmonious relationship between foreign investors and host states.

© Zhejiang University Press 2020

G. Wang et al., *Dispute Resolution Mechanism for the Belt and Road Initiative*,
https://doi.org/10.1007/978-981-15-1975-8

The rulings laid down by tribunals are only binding to the parties to the case, and do not have any precedential value. Besides, the rulings laid down by different tribunals vary, since different proceedings are adjudicated by different arbitrators. Investment arbitration often involves significant economic stakes and complex legal and factual issues. *Ad hoc* panels are constituted with no more than three individuals to scrutinize critical government decisions having important policy implications. Critics have also highlighted the risk associated with such a process that may lead to the rendering of a flawed or incompatible award, on a similar set of facts.

Also, there have been instances of domestic courts interfering in the enforcement of arbitral laws, and in the process, defeating the very purpose of international arbitration. This is compounded by a lack of an adequate, effective recourse to an appellate mechanism.

The issue could be addressed by the establishment of an appellate mechanism, as there would be a qualified tribunal to review arbitral awards on the basis of internationally accepted standards, instead of review by local courts which are vulnerable to government influences.

A. **Rationale for Creating an Appellate Mechanism**

There is increasing interest to have awards in investor-state cases under investment treaties to be made subject to a mechanism for the appeal of awards. Several treaties envisage, in broad terms, the eventual creation of such a mechanism. Instead of setting up separate *ad hoc* appellate mechanisms under separate agreements, setting up one single institutionally managed appellate mechanism (consisting of rules and procedures accepted by all) would perhaps be more prudent. The practicality of setting up an appellate mechanism should not be overlooked. A single institutional appellate mechanism will result in the reduction in the possibility of reaching conflicting conclusions, thereby increasing transparency and consistency. However, some sort of agreement needs to be reached amongst governments, investors, and other interested parties, with respect to structural and procedural concerns.

B. **Elements/Features of an Appellate Mechanism**

Taking into account the ICSID rules and other relevant international arbitration dispute rules, adoption of a WTO appellate body-style mechanism in a modified manner may be appropriate. This will help avoid the various legal and practical impediments inherent in setting up such an appellate mechanism.

The mechanism must be designed to provide coherence to the interpretation of trade and investment decisions. In so doing, it should take into account the following issues, among others:

- Transparency of proceedings of the mechanism;
- The applicable scope and standard of review;
- The nature and composition of the appellate mechanism;

- The effect of decisions by mechanism;
- The relationship of review by the appellate mechanism to the arbitral rules that may be selected;
- The relationship of review by the appellate mechanism to existing domestic laws and international law on enforcement of arbitral awards.

Some general comments on three of the major and fundamental issues relating to transparency, scope and standard of review, and nature and composition of the members of the mechanism, are as follows:

Transparency

Confidentiality of proceedings is a tradition and remains a common provision in bilateral investment treaties and many free trade agreements. However, given the interest of civil society groups in investment proceedings today, and states' obligations for transparency in matters that affect its laws and regulations, appellate mechanism for investment disputes may have to be open to the public. This does not necessarily mean that non-parties have to be in the same room during hearings. Reports/awards would have to be published (with provisions made for the protection of proprietary information).

Another important question that needs to be addressed is what right would there be to submit amicus curiae briefs. This can be accommodated but it should be at the appellate mechanism's discretion. What would be of greater concern from the perspective of effective transparency is establishing a system that ensures/enforces that transparency procedures are effective—such as uploading on Internet sites of the briefs, decisions and awards.

Scope and Standard of Review

The decision on the scope of the appellate mechanism's mandate and its standard of review is perhaps the most difficult of all. These elements are more challenging to address from a domestic perspective. What exactly does the appellate mechanism review—legal, or factual error, or both? Will its decisions be binding? Would be it be competent to hear appeals in all ICSID cases or only in some ICSID cases brought under treaties specifically provided for a two-level structure? Will it have the legal principle of determining points in litigation according to the precedent?

Nature and Composition of the Members of the Mechanism

The principal question with respect to the nature and composition of the members of the mechanism is whether there should be a "standing body" as with the WTO Appellate Body, or something similar to the ICSID *Ad Hoc* Annulment Committees, or similar to the ICC International Court of Arbitration.

The appeal of a standing body is of course, the sense of permanence, and therefore, the expectation of consistency and better quality awards/decisions because of the commitment. At the same time, the permanence of a standing body can be negative, as permanence may lead to exceeding the mandate—a body that sees itself to be an independent entity, rather than a servant of the parties.

The Belt and Road Initiative will be dealing with a limited group of countries—many of them are developing countries, and they may be wary of "international" bodies telling them how to regulate. In these circumstances, it would be appropriate to start with a roster system. From a cost perspective, it is also more economical, and it has the added benefit of being adaptable to a more permanent system if necessary.

With respect to the numerical element of the appellate mechanism's composition, what should be the appropriate number of members constituting the tribunal? The appropriate number of members constituting the tribunal should not be too large as the subject matter scope is fairly limited.

The members of the appellate mechanism roster should meet certain minimum standards—expertise in investment policy, and/or in investor-state arbitration and in international trade. There should also be a stringent, constantly reviewed code of conduct ensuring impartiality and the highest moral character.

Appendix 7
The Belt and Road Dispute Mechanism Proposal for Appellate Tribunal Rules

Basil Bitas

Introduction and Rationale

The Belt and Road dispute settlement mechanism is being proposed as a comprehensive dispute resolution tool for commercial, investor-state and state–state disputes. An appeal mechanism is proposed within this mechanism to provide certainty, coherence and consistency in decisions arising from the mechanism. A common argument that has been raised against the prevailing investor-state arbitration awards is that there is a lack of consistency in jurisprudence, given that there is no over-arching appeal authority which can make corrective or clarifying decisions and statements. In the ICSID system, an annulment procedure exists but its function is not an appellate one (even though some argue that recent annulment committees have, in effect, been attempting to play such a role).

In the area of B&R cross-border commercial disputes (private party–private party, or private party–state non-treaty disputes), such an appellate mechanism is not necessary, as finality—consistent with international commercial arbitration legislative practice—is key. This is indeed the case under, for example, the UNCITRAL Model Law regime. Hence, B&R appeal rules should address appeals arising from B&R disputes in the context of investor-state and state–state disputes.

Core Matters for the B&R Appellate Mechanism

It is recommended that such rules address the following core matters, in order to have a credible and strong system:

1. The name of the appeal tribunal;
2. The composition of the appeal tribunal: the number of members, qualifications, nationalities (e.g. regional representation requirements), appointment process, re-appointment process (if any);
3. The structure of tribunal (chair/president etc., how many will hear a case etc.);
4. The scope of appeal and appeal procedure: What matters may be raised on appeal (fact, law, mixed fact and law, etc.), whether there are any prerequisites

© Zhejiang University Press 2020

G. Wang et al., *Dispute Resolution Mechanism for the Belt and Road Initiative*,
https://doi.org/10.1007/978-981-15-1975-8

before an appeal can be initiated (e.g. whether the mandatory mediation was complied with earlier, and whether any specific flaws with the arbitral award/process below should be mentioned as specific reasons where an appeal is permitted), power of remand.
5. The working procedures (whether it will set its own procedures etc.);
6. The method of decision (majority, consensus or other methods);
7. The requirement to state reasons for its decisions;
8. The powers of the appeal body and orders it is empowered to make (e.g. damages, interest, other remedies);
9. The timeframe for the appeal process;
10. The manner of remuneration and by whom;
11. The code of conduct/ethics.

1. The name of the appeal tribunal

Proposed B&R Article 1 Establishment of [Appeal Tribunal] and Covered Disputes

1. There shall be a permanent [appeal tribunal…].
2. These Rules shall apply only to awards of the [tribunal] on covered disputes.
3. For the purposes of Paragraph 2, covered disputes shall not include disputes:
   (a) Between private parties; and
   (b) Between a private party/parties and a [state party or state entity] which does not arise from a treaty obligation.

(*New*)

2. The composition of the appeal tribunal: number of members, qualifications, nationalities (e.g. regional representation requirements), appointment process, re-appointment process (if any).

Proposed B&R Article 2 Composition and Structure of [Appeal Tribunal]

1. A permanent [appeal tribunal] is hereby established to hear appeals from the awards issued by the [tribunal].
2. The [appeal tribunal] shall be composed of [six] members, of whom [two] shall be nationals [of a member state of the European Union], [two] shall

be nationals of [the United States] and [two] shall be [nationals of third countries].

Source: EU TTIP draft

3. The parties, by decision of the […] Committee, shall, upon the entry into force of this agreement, appoint the members of the [appeal tribunal]. For this purpose, each party shall propose [three candidates], [two] of which may be nationals of [that party] and one shall be a non-national, for the […] committee to thereafter jointly appoint the members.

Source: EU TTIP draft

4. The [appeal tribunal] members shall be appointed for a [six-year] term, [renewable once[29]. However, the terms of three of the six persons appointed immediately after the entry into force of the agreement, to be determined by lot, shall extend to nine years.] Vacancies shall be filled as they arise. A person appointed to replace a person whose term of office has not expired shall hold office for the remainder of the predecessor's term.

Source: EU TTIP draft

5. The members of the [appeal tribunal] shall possess the [qualifications required in their respective countries for appointment to the highest judicial offices, or be jurists of recognized competence. They shall have demonstrated expertise in public international law.] It is [desirable] that they have expertise in international investment law, international trade law and the resolution of disputes arising under international investment or international trade agreements.

Source: EU TTIP draft
Alternative/additional wording for consideration from the WTO system:
The [Appellate Body] shall comprise persons of recognized authority, with demonstrated expertise in law, international trade and the subject matter of the covered agreements generally. They shall be unaffiliated with any government. The [Appellate Body] membership shall be broadly representative of membership [in the WTO]. All persons serving on the [Appellate Body] shall be available at all times and on short notice, and shall stay abreast of dispute settlement activities and other relevant activities of the [WTO]. They shall not participate in the consideration of any disputes that would create a direct or indirect conflict of interest.

[29]Current difficulties faced in the WTO Appellate Body process (May 2016) require B&R countries to consider whether to include the possibility of re-appointment.

3. Structure of Tribunal (Chair/President etc., how many will hear a case etc.)

6. The [appeal tribunal] shall have a [president and vice president] who shall be selected [by lot] for a [two-year] term and shall be selected [from among the members who are nationals of third countries]. They shall serve on the basis of a [rotation drawn by lot by the Chair of the […] Committee. The vice-president shall replace the president when the President is unavailable.

   Source: EU TTIP draft

7. The [appeal tribunal] shall hear appeals in divisions consisting of three members of whom one shall be a national of [a member state of the European Union, one a national of Vietnam and one a national of a third country]. The division shall be chaired by the member who is a national of [a third country].

   Source: EU-Vietnam FTA Art. 10

4. Scope of Appeal and Appeal Procedure: what matters may be raised on appeal (fact, law, mixed fact and law etc.); whether there are any pre-requisites before an appeal can be initiated (e.g. whether the mandatory mediation was complied with earlier, and whether any specific flaws with the arbitral award/process below should be mentioned as specific reasons where an appeal is permitted), power of remand.

Proposed B&R Article 3 Scope of Appeal and Appeal Procedure
An appeal shall be limited to [issues of law] covered in the [panel report] and legal interpretations developed by the [panel].

Source: The WTO

Proposed:

1. Either the disputing party may appeal before the [appeal tribunal] a provisional award, within [90 days] of its issuance. The grounds for appeal are:

   (a) That the tribunal has erred in the interpretation or application of the applicable law;
   (b) That the tribunal has manifestly erred in the appreciation of the facts, including the appreciation of relevant domestic law; or,
   (c) Those as provided for in Article 52 of the ICSID Convention, in so far as they are not covered by (a) and (b).

2. The appeal tribunal shall reject the appeal where it finds that the appeal is unfounded. It may also dismiss the appeal on an expedited basis where it is clear that the appeal is manifestly unfounded.
3. If the appeal tribunal finds that the appeal is well founded, the decision of the appeal tribunal shall modify or reverse the legal findings and conclusions in the provisional award in whole or part. Its decision shall specify precisely how it has modified or reversed the relevant findings and conclusions of the tribunal.

New B&R proposed provision:

4. An appeal on matters in Paragraph 1 of this article shall be carried out on a de novo basis.
5. Where the facts established by the [tribunal] so permit, the [appeal tribunal] shall apply its own legal findings and conclusions to such facts and render a final decision on the matter. Where this is not possible, it shall refer the matter back to the tribunal.
6. A disputing party lodging an appeal shall provide security, including the costs of appeal, as well as a reasonable amount determined by the appeal tribunal in light of the circumstances of the case.

Source: EU TTIP draft.

7. As a general rule, the appeal proceedings shall not exceed [180] days from the date a party to the dispute formally notifies its decision to appeal to the date the [appeal tribunal] issues its decision. When the [appeal tribunal] considers that it cannot issue its decision within [180] days, it shall inform the disputing parties in writing of the reasons for the delay together with an estimate of the period within which it will issue its decision. In no case should the proceedings exceed [270] days.
8. The provisions of Articles 11 [Third Party Funding], 20 [Transparency], 21 [Interim Decisions], 23 [Discontinuance] and 25 [The Non-Disputing Party] shall apply *mutatis mutandis* in respect of the appeal procedure.

Source: EU-Vietnam FTA Art. 28 (except for proposed Paragraph 7).

Proposed B&R Article 4 Final Award

1. A provisional award issued pursuant to this section shall become final if neither disputing party has appealed the provisional award pursuant to [Article 28 (1)].
2. Where a provisional award has been appealed and the [appeal tribunal] has rejected or dismissed the appeal pursuant to [Article 28(2)], the provisional award shall become final on the date of rejection or dismissal of the appeal by the [appeal tribunal].

3. Where a provisional award has been appealed and the [appeal tribunal] has rendered a final decision on the matter, the provisional award as modified or reversed by the [appeal tribunal] shall become final on the date of the issuance of the final decision of the [appeal tribunal].
4. Where a provisional award has been appealed and the [appeal tribunal] has modified or reversed the legal findings and conclusions of the provisional award and referred the matter back to the [tribunal], the [tribunal] shall, after hearing the disputing parties if appropriate, revise its provisional award to reflect the findings and conclusions of the [appeal tribunal]. The [tribunal] shall be bound by the findings made by the [appeal tribunal]. The [tribunal] shall seek to issue its revised award within [90] days of receiving the report of the [appeal tribunal]. The revised provisional award will become final award [90] days after its issuance.
5. For the purposes of this section, the term "final award" shall include any final decision of the appeal tribunal rendered pursuant to Article 28 (4).

Source: EU-Vietnam FTA Art. 29.

5. Working Procedures (whether it will set its own procedures etc.)

Proposed B&R Article 5 Working Procedures

The appeal tribunal shall draw up its own working procedures.

Source: EU TTIP draft.

6. Method of Decision (majority, consensus or other methods.)

Proposed B&R Article 6 Decision-Making

1. The [appeal tribunal] shall hear appeals in divisions consisting of three members of whom [one shall be a national of a member state of the European Union, one a national of Vietnam and one a national of a third country]. The division shall be chaired by the member who is a [national of a third country].
2. A division of the [appeal tribunal] shall make every effort to make any decision by consensus. Where, nevertheless, a decision cannot be arrived at by consensus, a division of the [appeal tribunal] shall render its decision by a majority of votes of all its members. Opinions expressed by individual members of a division of [appeal tribunal] shall be anonymous.

Source: EU-Vietnam FTA Art. 135.

New proposed B&R provision

3. The decision shall deal with every question submitted to the appeal [tribunal], and shall state the reasons upon which it is based.

   Adapted from ICSID Convention, Art. 48.

New proposed B&R provision

4. In the interpretation of the [Agreement/Treaty from which the dispute arises], regard is to be had to its international character and to the need to promote uniformity and certainty in interpretation.

   Adapted from UN CISG Art. 7.
   AND/OR
   The [appeal tribunal] shall interpret such [an agreement/a treaty] in accordance with the Vienna Convention on the Law of Treaties to promote uniformity and certainty.
   (New)

7. Manner of Remuneration and by Whom

Proposed B&R Article 7 Remuneration

1. The members of the appeal tribunal shall be paid a monthly retainer fee and receive a fee for each day working as a member, to be determined by decision of the […] Committee. [Note: the retainer and daily fee suggested by the EU would be around the same as for the WTO appeal tribunal members (i.e. a retainer fee of around 7,000 euros per month).]
2. The remuneration of the members shall be paid equally by both parties into an account managed by the Secretariat of [ICSID/the Permanent Court of Arbitration]. In the event that one party fails to pay the retainer fee the other party may elect to pay. Any such arrears will remain payable, with appropriate interest.
3. Upon a decision by the […] Committee, the retainer fee and the fees for days worked may be permanently transformed into a regular salary. In such an event, the members of the appeal tribunal shall serve on a full time basis and the […] Committee shall fix their remuneration and related organizational matters. In that event, the members shall not be permitted to engage in any occupation, whether gainful or not, unless exemption is exceptionally granted by the President of the appeal tribunal.

4. The Secretariat [ICSID/the Permanent Court of Arbitration] shall act as Secretariat for the appeal tribunal and provide it with appropriate support. The expenses for such support shall be met by the parties to the agreement equally.

Source: EU TTIP draft.

Printed by Printforce, United Kingdom